Joseph Ward

**The hand of Providence as shown in the history of nations and individuals**

From the great apostasy to the restoration of the Gospel

Joseph Ward

**The hand of Providence as shown in the history of nations and individuals**
*From the great apostasy to the restoration of the Gospel*

ISBN/EAN: 9783337281748

Printed in Europe, USA, Canada, Australia, Japan

Cover: Foto ©Thomas Meinert / pixelio.de

More available books at **www.hansebooks.com**

# THE HAND OF

# PROVIDENCE,

## AS SHOWN IN THE

## HISTORY OF

## NATIONS AND INDIVIDUALS,

From the Great Apostasy to the Restoration
of the Gospel.

————◆▶◀◆————

## ILLUSTRATED

————◆●◆————

BY ELDER J. H. WARD.

————

*SALT LAKE CITY, UTAH:*
Published at the Juvenile Instructor Office.
1883.

# PREFACE.

D ON'T throw this book down carelessly. It will do you no harm. It assumes no dictation. It may benefit you if you will read it carefully.

"We have plenty of histories."

True. But most are too large to be of practical value to the sons and daughters of toil. Many are written in the interest of some party or sect, and in order to gain favor, they flatter the vanity of men.

"But they tell of wonderful deeds, and thrilling adventures."

Very true. Some of them are mostly composed of recitals of legalized slaughter, and praise of tyrants who have climbed to power over the mangled bodies of their fellow-men, and whose names will not live in one grateful memory; while the real benefactors of the race, the unfolding of new and higher truths and, above all, the over-ruling hand of God are unnoticed, or, at most, barely mentioned.

"Does God rule the world?"

Yes, verily. The greatest actors on the theatre of the world are only instruments in the hand of God, for the execution of His purposes.

"Where have you obtained the facts contained in this volume?"

From many authentic works, some of them not easily accessible to most readers.

"This will be a good book for the young, and all those who have not the opportunity to consult larger works, will it not?"

With this idea it has been written and to this end I dedicate it to my children as heirs in the kingdom of God, to the youth of Zion and to my earnest friends everywhere.

THE AUTHOR.

Salt Lake City,
        March 16th, 1883.

# CONTENTS.

# ·THE HAND OF PROVIDENCE.

## CHAPTER I.

## THE DESTRUCTION OF JERUSALEM AND APOSTASY OF THE EARLY CHURCH.

INJUSTICE OF ROMAN GOVERNORS—NERO EMPEROR—VES-
PASIAN AND TITUS SENT TO JUDEA—FORTIFICATIONS OF
JERUSALEM—TITUS OFFERS TERMS OF PEACE—HORRORS
OF THE SIEGE—WOMEN DEVOUR THEIR OWN CHILDREN
—TEMPLE BURNED—CITY DESTROYED—DISPERSION OF
THE JEWS—UNIVERSAL APOSTASY—PRIESTHOOD NO MORE
—IDEAS OF GOD PREVERTED—WORSHIP CORRUPTED WITH
HEATHEN RITES — PERSECUTION OF CHRISTIANS —
EMPEROR CONSTANTINE—RISE OF MONASTIC ORDER.

ACCORDING to the best records that have come down to us, the last book of the New Testament (commonly called the Apocalypse of St. John) was written about sixty years after the ascension of our Savior.

At that time the gospel of Jesus Christ had been preached in all the principal cities and countries of the known world. Numerous branches of the primitive church had been planted in Palestine, Syria, Egypt, Asia Minor, Greece and Italy.

In the meantime the awful doom which the Savior predicted against Jerusalem had been literally fulfilled. Shortly after the crucifixion and ascension of the Savior, Judea became the theatre of many cruelties and oppressions arising from contentions between the Jewish priests, the depredations of numerous bands of robbers, which infested the country; but more than all from the injustice and avarice of the Roman governors.

*1*

The last of these governors, was Gessius Florus, whom
Josephus represents as a monster in wickedness and cruelty,
and whom the Jews regarded rather as a bloody executioner,
sent to torture, than as a magistrate to govern them.

During the government of Felix, his predecessor, a dispute
having arisen between the Jews and Syrians about the city of
Cæsarea, their respective claims were referred to the emperor,
Nero, at Rome.    The decision was in favor of the Syrians,
and the Jews immediately took up arms to avenge their
cause.

In this state of things, Nero gave orders to Vespasian to march into Judea with a powerful army. Accordingly, Vespasian, accompanied by his son Titus, marched into Palestine at the head of 60,000 well-disciplined troops. While Vespasian was thus preparing more effectually to curb the still unbroken spirit of the Jews, intelligence arrived of the death of the emperor and his own election to the throne. Departing therefore for Rome he left the best of his troops with his son, ordering him to besiege and utterly destroy Jerusalem.

Titus lost no time in carrying into effect his father's injunction. Jerusalem was strongly fortified both by nature and art. Three walls surrounded it which were considered impregnable; besides which it had numerous towers outside of the walls, lofty, firm and strong. The circumference was nearly four miles.

Desirous of saving the city, Titus repeatedly sent offers of peace to the inhabitants; but they were indignantly rejected. At length finding all efforts at treaty ineffectual, he entered upon the siege determined not to leave it until he had razed the city to its foundation.

The internal state of the city soon became horrible. The inhabitants being divided in their counsels fought with one another, and the streets were often deluged with blood shed by the hands of kindred. In the meantime famine spread its horrors abroad, and pestilence its ravages. Thousands died daily and were carried out of the gates to be buried at the public expense; until being unable to hurry them to the grave the wretched victims were thrown into houses as fast as they fell, and there shut up.

During the prevalence of the famine, the house of a certain woman by the name of Miriam was repeatedly plundered of such provisions as she had been able to procure. So extreme did her suffering become, that she entreated those around her, to put an end to her miserable existence. At length frantic with fury and despair she snatched her infant from her bosom, killed and cooked it; and having satiated her present hunger, concealed the rest. The smell of food soon drew the voracious human tigers to her house; they threatened her with tortures she hid her provisions from them. Being thus compelled

she set before them the relics of her mangled babe. At the
sight of this horrid spectacle, inhuman as they were, they
stood aghast, petrified with horror, and at length rushed precipitately from the house.

When the report of this spread through the city, the con-
sternation was universal and inexpressible. The people now,
for the first time, began to think themselves forsaken of God.
In the mind of Titus the recital awakened both horror and
indignation, and he resolved to push the siege with still greater
vigor, aiming particularly to obtain possession of the temple.
The preservation of this noble edifice was strongly desired by
him; but one of the Roman soldiers being exasperated by the
Jews, or, as Josephus says, "pushed on by the hand of Providence," seized a blazing firebrand, and getting on his comrades'
shoulders, threw it through a window, and soon the whole north
side was in a flame. Titus immediately gave order to extin-
guish the fire; but the enraged soldiers, bent on destroying the
city and all it contained, either did not hear or did not regard
him. The flames continued to spread until this consecrated
edifice, the glory of the nation, became one mingled heap of
ruins. Then followed a terrible massacre in which thousands
perished, some in the flames and others by the sword of the
enemy. At length the city was abandoned to the fury of the
soldiers. It is said that nearly one million five hundred
thousand persons perished in the siege.

The conquest of the city being achieved, Titus proceeded to ·
demolish its noble structures, its fortifications, palaces and walls.
So literally were the predictions of the Savior fulfilled respect-
ing its destruction that not one stone was left upon another
that was not thrown down.

From that day the Jews have been dispersed through the
world, despised and hated, persecuted and yet upheld—lost as
it were among the nations, and yet distinct—they live as the
monuments of the truth of God.

While the apostles lived the churches planted by them continued to exist with more or less of spiritual life.

But the spirit of apostasy was already at work. In some
places pagan rites and ceremonies had perverted the worship
of the true God and but few could be found who remained

pure amid the corruptions of the age or undaunted by the
trials and persecutions that surrounded them on every side.

So universal was this apostasy that only seven churches
throughout Asia, Africa and Europe were considered worthy
of being either reproved or blessed by the voice of revelation.
(*See Revelations 2nd and 3rd chapters.*)

The whole eastern continent of which we have authentic
history was at that period under the control of Rome, and
paganism was the religion of the empire.    Thus the whole
power of the realm was brought to bear against the infant
church.

Pagan priests excited the populace to frenzy, and royal
decrees delivered the saints to the most terrible tortures and
death.

In a few years the apostolic organization and priesthood
were no more.  A few glimmerings of spiritual light remained
for a short time, among those who had taken refuge in the
catacombs or subterranean vaults of Rome, or had fled to the
wilds of the Libyan desert.   But even this light was soon
extinguished, and then fell that mental, moral, and spirituul
night from which mankind are only now slowly emerging.

But false religion could never satisfy the cravings of the
immortal soul.

Paganism presented only a cheerless prospect.   It gave
itself no concern for the lowly and unfortunate, limited the
hopes and destiny of man to this present life, and taught him
that temporal prosperity might be selfishly gained at any cost
to others in property and suffering.   For example, Rome, for
many ages had enriched herself with the wealth of conquered
nations, and impoverished them that her sons and daughters
might live in luxury and grandeur.   Yet throughout her vast
dominions there were no institutions of benevolence; no hospitals for the sick, no asylums for the afflicted or unfortunate.
The pleasant pastimes of her populace were to witness scenes
of cruelty; and the most refined ladies of that period eagerly
thronged the amphitheatres to view the agonies of captives
from distant tribes or early Christian martyrs as they were
thrown to famished and enraged wild beasts in the public
arena.   Many of the early Christains were thus put to death

in the Coliscum, the ruins of which are shown in the engraving.

No wonder then that when the church was taken from the earth, and its forms amalgamated with pagan institutions, the world presented an unparalleled scene of carnage and cruelty, bloodshed and terror.

But Rome. was destined to endure a terrible retribution. The northern barbarians whom she had so long oppressed, and from whom she had drawn many of the victims of her gladiatorial combats now wreaked their long-sought vengeance, spreading terror and devastation wherever they went.

One of them, Attila, king of the Huns, called himself the scourge of God, and boasted that grass never grew where his horse had trodden. These incursions spread an intellectual famine throughout Europe. The only men of learning were the monks, who seldom left their cloisters, and the only books were manuscripts concealed in the libraries of the monasteries. Not only were the common people extremely ignorant, but also the rich and noble, and even the kings could scarcely read or write. The reign of superstition was universal. The simplicity of primitive worship was changed to an unmeaning round of rites and ceremonies: and the glorious principles of the gospel were hidden from sight by a dark cloud of ignorance, mysticism and unintelligible jargon, out of which there too often flashed the lurid lightenings of priestly vengeance and persecutions.

The Lord, speaking by the mouth of Jeremiah, says, "My people have committed two errors; they have forsaken me, the fountain of living waters and hewed them out cisterns, broken cisterns that can hold no water." When the voice of revelation was hushed men began to follow fables and traditions, and he who possessed the livliest imagination invented the greatest number.

They, instead of the word of God, became the rule of life; and men sought by bodily suffering to purchase admission to the courts of heaven.

We pity the devotee of India, who measures by the length of his body, the wearisome journey of hundreds of miles; or the fakir who sits with his legs in an upright position, for years until the limbs becomes withered, distorted and useless. But what shall we say of a professed follower of the Savior who makes a pilgrimage of a thousand miles with sharp spikes driven into the inside of his shoes, by which his feet are lacer-

FAKIR.

ated at every step!   Or of one who spends the greater part of his life sitting on a column thirty feet high and only three feet in diameter, through all the vicissitudes of the seasons, storm and sunshine, cold and heat, with the idea that, by this means, he could secure salvation and exaltation in the presence of God!   Surely it was the self-same pagan idea that actuated all.

In those days, also, even the forms and ceremonies of the primitive church underwent complete transformation.   Pagan rites were celebrated at Christian festivals, and days commemorative of great events were made to conform to the times appointed for the worship of heathen divinities.

For example, the festival of Easter as observed by the Catholic church, was and still is degraded by pagan rites. And the day that commemorates our Savior's birth, which event took place in April, when the shepherds were abroad on the plains of Bethlehem, with their flocks, was changed from the beautiful Spring time to the dark and gloomy December, that it might conform to a day already set apart for pagan ceremonies, and by this means was secured its universal observance.

The ideas concerning God were also perverted.   Space will permit only a glance at this subject.   The passions that were said to control the character of heathen gods were attributed to the great Creator and loving Father of us all.   He was represented as delighting in vengeance; and glorying in the eternal sufferings of His creatures.   Thus the most inhuman persecutors claimed they were doing His will; and hence arose the doctrine of endless torments beyond the grave, which still disgraces nearly all the sects of Christendom.   The doctrine of fate has ever been a prominent doctrine of pagan religions.

This dogma was also engrafted into their creed; hence, we find learned teachers of the present age gravely asserting that, owing to the unalterable decrees of God, there are young and irresponsible infants, scarcely a span in length, who are and ever will be doomed to suffer the torments of the lost.

Such was the condition of the social and religious world at the time of the Emperor Constantine.

This politic prince was not a man of religious convictions, but hoping to consolidate his power and gain vast numbers of adherents he granted universal religious toleration and even went so far as to proclaim himself a Christian.

This act of toleration gave a temporary protection to all classes and was of especial benefit to those who wished to retire from the confusion and corruption of the age, and spend their lives in pursuit of science, literature and philosophy.

Such were the tasteless and often brutal amusements, the low sensuality, the base intrigue and bloody warfare of those times, that many longed for retirement and seclusion.

Men and also women, sometimes of the highest rank, awoke, suddenly to the discovery that life was given them for nobler purposes.

Loathing society, despising themselves, and often their companions, to whom they had been wedded in loveless marriages —companions whose infidelities and licentiousness they had too often to endure, they fled from a world which had sated and sickened them.

Thus arose the monastic order.

By the side of Alpine torrents and in the valleys of Piedmont, by the rocky shores of the beautiful Ægean sea and on its lonely yet lovely islands, as well as on the classic hillsides of Judea, arose thousands of monasteries.

At first, no doubt, the inmates sought for a higher and purer life; but after a time they too sunk into luxury, licentiousness and debauchery.

Yet these monastic institutions served one good purpose, and that one was important.   During these perilous times science and literature here found an asylum.   Libraries were formed and carefully preserved, which, on the restoration of learning, were of great value to the world.

The foregoing will indicate to some extent the condition of mankind at the close of the sixth century of the Christian era. The light of antiquity had perished.   The dawn of modern days had not yet gilded the eastern horizon.   The world presented over its whole surface one vast field of contention and bloodshed, with scarcely an object sufficiently prominent to excite interest or deserve attention.

It was the midnight hour of human history.

Though the early church had been destroyed and the priesthood taken from the earth; yet God did not give it up as lost, nor entirely withdraw His Spirit.    Then as now "the earth is the Lord's," and He will yet make good His claim to it.    It is a blood-bought world, and He who ransomed it at so dear a price will one day return to rule over it as King of kings and Lord of lords.    The earth that was bedewed with the Savior's tears and sweat—the earth that was trodden by His hallowed feet—the earth that drank His life blood shall yet throw off the curse that has so long blighted it and receive its paradisaic glory.

Through agencies the most diverse the minds of men were developed and disciplined for the reception of truth until in the Lord's due time in a prepared place and among a people prepared to receive His truth, He would again restore His priesthood, and set up His kingdom upon the earth.

# CHAPTER II.

## MAHOMET.

DESCRIPTION OF ARABIA—ARABIAN CUSTOMS—BIRTH OF
MAHOMET—EARLY LIFE—JOURNEY TO SYRIA—CHRISTIAN
SECTS—DOCTRINES TAUGHT BY MAHOMET—HIS MARRIAGE
—PROCLAIMS HIMSELF A PROPHET—PERSECUTION—FLEES
TO MEDINA—BECOMES POWERFUL—SICKNESS AND DEATH
—PERSONAL APPEARANCE.

FAR away in the south-western part of Asia, lies a strange
and peculiar country called Arabia. It is bounded on the
north by Syria, on the east by the Persian Gulf, on the south
by the Indian Ocean, and on the west by the Red Sea, and
comprises more than a million of square miles, or about twelve
times the area of Utah.

This vast region possesses a diversified landscape. In some
places vast sandy deserts stretch away farther than the eye can
reach; in others, immense piles of dark volcanic rock rear aloft
their barren peaks, around whose base the dry, hot winds have
drifted the sands of the desert for untold centuries. However,
in the secluded valleys of the mountains, and along the base
of the great mountain chains, may be found many fertile
tracts, where, watered by pure and never-failing mountain
streams, and warmed by the rays of a tropical sun, the earth
produces in abundance nearly every kind of grain, vegetable,
fruit, flower and aromatic shrub that can conduce to the happiness of man. Indeed, some portions are so wonderfully pro-
ductive, that in ancient as well as modern times it has received
the significant title of "Araby the blest."

Most of the inhabitants of this country are generally considered to be the descendants of Ishmael, the son of Abraham.
Many of them lead a wild, nomadic life, supported by their
flocks and herds and the spontaneous productions of the soil,

and retain among their laws and customs, many of the usages that prevailed in the primitive, patriarchal times of their great ancestor.

Others live in towns and cities and engage in commerce, either with foreign countries or with distant parts of their own land.

The usual method of transporting their merchandise is on the backs of camels, and sometimes several hundred or even a thousand of these animals, accompanied by their drivers, may be seen slowly wending their way across the desert, carrying with them the coffee of Mocha and spices of Muscat to the distant cities of Bagdad and Damascus.

As among the Jews the ruling priests were chosen from the tribe of Levi and family of Aaron, so, among the ancient Arabs, the guardians of the sacred things of their worship were chosen from the tribe of Koreish and family of Haschem.

Abd-Al-Mutallib was the ruling priest in Mecca, the sacred city of Arabia, at the time that his grandson, Mahomet, was born, which event occurred at Mecca, in the year 570 of the Christian era.

Of Mahomet's parents, but little is recorded, except that his father, Abdallah, was remarkable for his commanding presence and great personal beauty. He died when his future illustrious son was only two months old. Amina, his mother, who is said to have been of Jewish descent, also died when Mahomet was only six years old.

The early life of Mahomet was spent in the house of his Uncle, Abou Taleb, who had become the principal guardian of the Ca-aba, or great temple, of ancient Arabian worship.

The ceremonies and devotions connected with this temple-worship may have given an early bias to Mahomet's mind, and inclined it to those speculations and ideas in which it afterwards became engrossed. His education in childhood seems to have been neglected; for he was not taught either to read or write. But he was a thoughtful child, quick to observe, prone to meditate on all that he had observed, and possessed of an imagination fertile, daring and expansive.

At the age of twelve years, Mahomet solicited the privilege of accompanying his uncle, Abou Taleb, to Syria, whither he was about to conduct a caravan. Their route lay through regions fertile in fables and traditions, which it is the delight of the Arabs to recount in the evening halts of the caravan.

With an attentive ear, the youthful Mahomet listened to those tales of enchantment and wonderful events which happened in days of old, and doubtless imbibed ideas that had a powerful influence on him in his after life. In this journey also he listened to the conversation of many of those exiles from the Christian sects, who, in fleeing from persecution had taken refuge in the wilds of Northern Arabia. Thus he learned many facts concerning the Christian religion.

Having arrived at the city of Bozrah, which was situated on the confines of Syria, about seventy miles south of Damascus, Mahomet was entertained at a Nestorian convent. One of the monks named Bahira, was very much interested by the spirit of inquiry and intelligence which the youth manifested, especially on religious subjects, and gave him all possible information.

Mahomet returned to Mecca, his imagination teeming with the wild tales and traditions picked up in the desert, and his mind deeply impressed with the teachings he had received among the Nestorians.

In order that we may understand the nature of the teachings which Mahomet received on this and subsequent journeys to Syria, an enumeration of the leading dogmas of the jarring sects of oriental Christians will be necessary :

The most numerous of these sects were the Arians, so called from Arius, a great religious teacher of Alexandria. They claimed that Jesus Christ was the Son of God, the Father; that His existence commenced at His advent in this world; that He was created for a special mission, but was subject to the influences of virtue and vice like common mortals.

The followers of Nestorius, the great bishop of Constantinople, were also very numerous; and Mahomet, in his subsequent journeys to Syria, frequently came in contact with them. They claimed that Christ had two distinct natures, human and divine; that Jesus was a man; that Mary was only His mother according to the flesh, and that it was an abomination to style her "Mary the mother of God," as was and still is the custom of the Catholic church.

Another sect was the Marianites, or worshipers of Mary. They regarded the trinity as consisting of God, the eternal Father, Mary, the eternal mother, and Christ, their Son.

The Valentinians were another sect, who taught -that Jesus Christ was only a wise and virtuous mortal, selected by God to reform and instruct mankind. Their creed is still professed by some of the Unitarian sects of the present day.

The Nazarenes were a sect of Jewish Christians, who considered Christ as the promised Messiah, but conformed in all other respects to the rites and ceremonies of the Mosaic law.

Many other sects might be enumerated who took their names from learned and zealous leaders, and who were subdivided into various and opposing parties of fanatical enthusiasts.

A glance at these dissentions which convulsed society at this period is sufficient to acquit Mahomet of any charge of conscious blasphemy in the opinions he taught concerning the nature and mission of our Savior.

The principal doctrines taught by Mahomet were drawn from the writings of the Old and New Testaments. He recognized in all about three hundred prophets. This number included all the ancient worthies of the Old Testament, as well as the Savior and the apostles, evangelists and martyrs mentioned in the New. However, four persons were considered as greater prophets than the rest, and were reverenced as the founders of four distinct dispensations. These were Abraham, Moses, Jesus and Mahomet.

The book containing the writings and revelations of Mahomet is commonly called the Koran. However, Mahomet should not be held responsible for all that the Koran contains, as there is abundant evidence that it has been changed and corrupted in many places since his death.

Prayer, fasting and acts of charity are inculcated by it. Merchants were especially commanded to perform acts of charity, as they were the class who were most liable to the sins

of deception and extortion. The creed which all were required
to believe, was simply, "There is one God, and Mahomet is
His prophet."

But little is known of Mahomet's history between his twelfth
and twenty-fifth year. He seems to have been engaged prin-
cipally in conducting caravans across the desert. He thereby
gained much practical knowledge, and became known as a
young man of ability and integrity, pleasing appearance, and
engaging manners.

At the age of twenty-five, he became the steward or business
agent of a certain wealthy widow, named Cadijah; and a few
years later she married him and faithfully followed him till
her death, through all the vicissitudes of his strange and
eventful life.

When Mahomet, in his fortieth year, proclaimed himself the
prophet of God, Cadijah replied, "I will be thy first believer."
They knelt down in prayer together.

Twelve centuries have passed since then, and nine thousand
millions of human beings have followed her example.

We are told that as Mahomet lay wrapped in his mantle,
in the silent watches of the night, he heard a voice calling
upon him. Uncovering his head, a flood of light burst
upon him of such intolerable splendor that he swooned
away.

On regaining his senses, he beheld an angel, who, approaching him from a distance, displayed a scroll, covered with written
characters. "Read," said the angel.

"I know not how to read," replied Mahomet.

"Read," repeated the angel, "in the name of God, who has
created all things."

Upon this, Mahomet instantly felt his understanding
illumined, and read what was written. These words were afterwards promulgated in the Koran, which also contains many of
the doctrines taught in the New Testament.

When he had finished reading, the heavenly messenger
announced, "O, Mahomet, verily thou art a prophet of God,
and I am His angel Gabriel."

Mahomet, we are told, came trembling and agitated to
Cadijah in the morning, and told her what he had seen and

heard. She saw everything with the eye of faith, and embraced those teachings with the devotion of an affectionate woman.

"Joyful tidings dost thou bring!" exclaimed she. "By Him in whose hand is the soul of Cadijah, I henceforth regard thee as the prophet of our nation. Rejoice! rejoice! Allah will not suffer thee to come to shame. Hast thou not been loving to thy kindred, kind to thy neighbors, charitable to the poor, hospitable to the stranger, faithful to thy word, and ever a defender of the truth?"

The announcement of Mahomet's message provoked bitter opposition among his kindred. Only one of them, his cousin Ali, became his disciple. Those who had known him from his infancy, who had seen him a boy about the streets of Mecca, and afterwards engaged in the ordinary concerns of life, scoffed at the idea of his assuming the prophetic character. When he walked the streets he was subjected to jeers and insults. If he attempted to preach, his voice was drowned by discordant noises and ribald songs. As gradually his followers increased, so did the opposition in bitterness and intensity.

At length he was obliged to flee from his native city and take refuge in Medina, a city of north-western Arabia.

Space will not permit a recital of the numerous intrigues of his enemies, or his various successes. Suffice it to say that, in a few years he became the leader of a powerful, constantly-increasing and enthusiastic people.

The time had at length arrived when the wild, wandering and discordant tribes of Arabia were to be marshalled under one banner, united in one creed and animated by one cause; when a mighty genius had arisen, who should bring together those scattered remnants, inspire them with his own religious zeal and daring spirit, and send them forth an invincible host, to shake and overturn the empires of the earth.

Mahomet survived the most of his children, and died in the sixty-third year of his age.

In his last illness, he gave his followers three parting commands: "Expel all idolaters from Arabia; allow every believer equal privileges with yourselves; devote yourselves to prayer and the propagation of the faith."

1*

When the hour of death approached he feared it not, but, gazing upwards with unmoving eyelids, he exclaimed, "O, Allah! be it so, forever with the glorious associates in paradise."

Thus passed away the man who gave embodiment to a faith that is still adhered to by more than 130,000,000 of the human family; and who founded an empire that was the most extensive the world has ever seen.

In appearance, he was of the middle stature. His head was capacious, and well set on a neck that rose like a pillar from his ample chest. He had an oval face, dark eyes, long, wavy hair and a full beard. His deportment was calm and dignified, and he is said to have possessed a smile of captivating sweetness. His complexion was fairer than Arabs usually are, and in his enthusiastic moments there was a glow and radiance to his countenance. He was extremely cleanly in his person, abstemious in his diet, and simple and unaffected in his dress and manners. He seemed to have an intuitive knowledge of human nature, and an innate power to counsel, command, reprove and inspire his followers with his own ardent nature. Take him all in all, the race has seldom seen a teacher more kind, more noble or more sincere.

# CHAPTER III.

## THE SARACENIC CONQUEST.

CAUSES OF TRIUMPHS—ABOU-BEKER ELECTED CALIPH—WAR
DECLARED—FALL OF BOZRAH—BATTLE OF AIZNADIN—
SIEGE OF JERUSALEM—DEPARTURE OF ROMAN EMPEROR
—SARACEN FLEET—EASTERN CONQUESTS—FALL OF ALEX-
ANDRIA—CONQUEST OF NORTHERN AFRICA—CONQUEST
OF SPAIN—BATTLE OF POICTIERS—EXTENT OF SARACEN
EMPIRE.

AFTER the death of Mahomet, his followers assumed the
name of Saracens, by which title they were afterwards
generally known. This term, it is said, is derived from two
Arabic words which signify eastern, or oriental, and conquerors.

Scarcely was Mahomet buried, when it was found necessary
to form a civil and political constitution and code of laws, by
which his followers were to be governed. This government was
called the Caliphate.

Mahometanism, even during the life of its founder, gave
unmistakable indications of overpassing the bounds of Arabia.

A few years later it entered upon a system of conquest
unparalleled in the history of the world.

One cause of this phenomenon is to be found in the moral
and social condition of the world. The influence of religion
had long before ceased. Christianity was completely paganized.
Her popes were busy denouncing and excommunicating each
other, in their rivalry for earthly power; or bribing royal
females and courtesans to influence the decision of councils,
that were supposed by the masses to speak with the voice of
God. Her bishops no longer sought to feed their flocks with
the bread of life. On the other hand they were concerned in
assassinations, poisonings, adulteries, roits, treason and civil

war.  The religious teachers of those days never raised their voices in the sacred cause of liberty, or spoke in defense of the outraged rights of man.

No wonder then that, in the midst of the wrangling of sects, and unintelligible jargon of Arians, Augustinians, Nestorians and Marianites, society stood in breathless awe, when it heard the terrible Arabian battle cry, "There is but one God, and Mahomet is His prophet!" enforced as it was by the tempest of Saracen armies.  These warriors, armed with lances and cimeters, and mounted on fleet Arabian steeds, passed swiftly from city to city, and frequently found the masses of the people so crushed by tyranny, so worn out by wrangling and civil wars, that they welcomed the Saracens as deliverers.

Mahomet's life had been almost entirely occupied in the conquest or conversion of his native country.  It is true, in the latter part of his career he felt himself strong enough to threaten Persia for the aid she had given his enemies; and he even declared war against the Roman Empire for the same reason.  But failing health frustrated his designs.  He had made no provision for the perpetuation of his own power. Hence, a struggle ensued before a successor was appointed. At length, Abou Beker, the father of his wife Ayesha, was selected.  He was proclaimed the first Caliph, and immediately attacked both the Romans and the Persians.

The reknowned general, Khaled, commonly called by Saracen historians, "the sword of God," was despatched into Syria. His name struck terror into the hearts of the inhabitants. The fortified town of Bozrah fell into his hands without a struggle.  This was the same town where fifty years previous the youthful Mahomet had been entertained at the Nestorian convent.  Marching northward seventy miles, to Damascus, Khaled laid siege to the Syrian capital.  A decisive battle took place on the plain of Aiznadin.  The Roman army was overthrown and dispersed.  A few days later Damascus surrendered to the Saracens.

Guarded on the right by the beautiful river Orontes, and on the left by the snow-clad peaks of Lebanon, they still continued their march northward.  To resist their further progress, the Roman emperor, Heraclius, collected an army of one hundred and forty thousand men. A great battle took place on the plains of Yermuck. At the first onset the Saracens were repulsed; but driven back to the field by the heroism of their women, who also aided them, they ended the conflict by the complete overthrow of the Roman army.

The whole of Syria now fell into the hands of the Saracens.

They then turned south and laid siege to the city of Jerusalem. After a defense of four months the patriarch, Sophronius, appeared on the wall and asked the terms of capitulation. It was stipulated that the surrender should take place in the pre-

DAMASCUS.

sence of the Caliph himself. Accordingly, he came all the way from Medina for that purpose. At that time such were the customs among the Saracens, that it is said the ambassador found the Caliph Omar asleep under the shadow of a mosque. It is also said that he journeyed alone on a red camel, carrying with him a bag of dates for his own food and one of corn for his camel, a wooden dish and a leathern water bottle.

After receiving the surrender of the city, Omar returned to Medina as quietly as he had come.

Thus fell the Roman power in Syria and Palestine, after having ruled those countries nearly eight hundred years. Thus was transferred without tumult or outrage the religious capital of the professedly Christian world into the hands of the Caliph Omar. Thus, Jerusalem, so long considered the birthplace of Christianity, the scene of its most sacred and tragic memories, passed into the hands of the Mahometans. Considerably more than a thousand years have elapsed since then, and it is still under their dominion. The mosque of Omar now rears its lofty minarets where once stood the temple of Solomon.

Heraclius, the Roman emperor, struggled valiantly to retain his possessions. He plainly saw that the corruptions of Christianity were among the causes of Saracenic triumphs. He made a heroic attempt to rouse the clergy to their duties, but it was then too late. Heraclius himself was obliged to seek safety in flight. From the deck of the little vessel that bore him homeward, he gazed intently on the receding hills, and in bitterness of anguish exclaimed, "Farewell, Syria, forever farewell!"

The remaining details of the Saracen conquest we need not here relate. The naming of their victories is sufficient to indicate the greatness of their triumphs.

The great cities of Tyre and Cæsarea were captured. With the cedars of Lebanon and sailors of Tyre they equipped a fleet that drove the Roman navy into the Hellespont. Thus they gained undisturbed control of the Mediterranean, and conquered or colonized the islands of Cyprus, Candia, Rhodes, Sicily, Sardinia, Corsica and many others. A "Saracen naval expedition even appeared before the walls of Rome, and after threatening the imperial city, carried away the altar of silver from St. Peter's church, and gathered other relics from the tombs of St. Peter and St. Paul.

One of the Saracen armies turned eastward, and on the battle-field of Cadesia the fate of Persia was decided. After the battle of Neha-vend the treasury and royal arms of Persia fell into the hands of the Saracens.

After this battle the eastern army divided into two divisions. One marched northward to the Caspian Sea and took possession of the neighboring countries; another, southward to Persepolis, from whence the king of Persia fled for his life across the dreary deserts of Khorassan. The name of Saracen terri-

fied the wild tribes of independent Tartary, and they hastened
to pay tribute and accept the faith of their conquerors.

The emperor of China, in his palace at Peking, heard of
their exploits, and sent ambassadors to them, craving their
friendship. The kingdoms now included in Afghanistan and
Beloochistan surrendered at their approach, and the
Mahometan standard of the crescent waved on the banks of
the Indus.

Meanwhile important events were transpiring in the west.
A large proportion of the Egyptian people welcomed the Saracens. The Arabs of the desert loitered in the palaces of the
ancient Pharaohs. Alexandria, aided by Roman troops, alone
held out. After a siege of fourteen months it also fell, and
with it Egypt and Abyssinia were added to the dominions of
the Caliphs.

The most powerful religious empire that the world has ever
seen had suddenly sprung into existence. It stretched from
the Great Wall of China to the burning sands of Tripoli, and
from the Caspian Sea on the north to Abyssinia on the south.
Yet this was but little more than half the territory that it
soon afterwards controlled. One of its armies advanced on
Constantinople. It did not fall then, but afterwards became
the capital of the Mahometan power in Europe. Another
took possession of the whole north of Africa, and, having
consolidated its power there, under the command of their
general, Tarik, they crossed the straits that separate Africa
from Spain, and landing on the rocky clift of Gib-el-Tarik, or
mountain of Tarik (now called Gibraltar), unfurled their green
banner with golden crescent for the first time on the soil of
Europe.

Tarik was soon followed into Spain by his superior officer,
the emir Musa. They took possession of the whole southern
portion of Spain and Portugal, which in their own picturesque
language, they named Andalusia, or the region of the
evening.

It was soon found that the whole peninsula was ripe for
revolution. The Jews comprised a large proportion of the
Spanish people. They were, to a great extent, the cultivators
of the soil, which pursuit well repaid their labors. They were

then, as now, famous as merchants and money-lenders, and many of them held high positions in the government, while thousands of them were scattered in every city, town and village, as the physicians and teachers of the people.

Their wrongs had been accumulating for centuries. Bigotry, envy and avarice had conspired to point them out as objects of persecution. Laws were passed which were never intended to be executed. It was expected that they would purchase a remission of the penalties by pouring their hard-earned treasures into the lap of Rome. No doubt the Jews exulted as the tide of Saracen conquest swept onward. They did not deplore a change of masters for those who would leave them in possession of civil and religious liberty.

Before long the whole Iberian peninsula fell into the hands of the Mahometans. Not content with this, they crossed the Pyrenees, and took possession of that portion of France that lies to the south of the river Loire. All Central France was overrun. Castles, churches and monasteries were despoiled. For a time they held undisturbed dominion. The empire of the Saracens was then at its greatest extent. It reached from the confines of China to the Atlantic ocean, and comprised within its limits forty degrees of latitude and nearly one hundred and twenty of longitude. In Western Europe alone it stretched in an unbroken line more than a thousand miles northward from the cliffs of Gibraltar. More than thirty-six thousand cities paid tribute to the successors of Mahomet in the city of Medina.

In attempting to extend their conquests northward the Saracens were met by an army under Charles Martel, king of France, A. D. 732. Between Tours and Poictiers a terrible battle was fought, which lasted seven days. The Franks and Goths lost so many that it was impossible to tell the number of the slain. But these losses were more than counterbalanced by the losses of the Saracens whose great general, Abderahman, was found among the slain. Their previous successes had filled them with pride. They looked with contempt upon their enemies. For example, when the Roman emperor, Nicephorous, had sent a threatening letter to the Caliph Haroun-al-Raschid, the latter replied, "In the name of the most merciful

God, Haroun-al-Raschid, commander of the faithful, to Nicephorous, the Roman dog! I have read thy letter, O thou son of an unbelieving mother! Thou shalt not hear my words; thou shalt behold my reply!'' A few weeks later it was written in letters of blood on the plains of Phrygia.

Although the Saracen empire had reached the zenith of its power, in one sense Mahometanism had not reached it's culmination. The day was to come, when under the name of Ottoman Turks, it would expel the descendants of the Cæsars from their capital, hold the classic land of Greece in subjection, and under the very walls of Vienna dispute the empire of Europe in the center of that continent; and in Africa extend its dogmas and faith across burning deserts and pestilential forests far south of the equinoctial line.

It is a mistaken idea that the progress of the Saracens depended on the sword alone. The causes of their success were many and various. One of these, the paganization of Christianity, has already been noticed. The long and desolating wars of the Romans had thrown the whole oriental and African trade into the hands of the Arabs. Hence a commercial interest and sympathy had grown up between these peoples. Another reason was the mildness of the Saracen government in comparison with that of the Romans. The only taxation was a single annual tribute, amounting to less than one-half the various taxes by the Romans. Another feature was complete religious toleration except to idolators. The only creed required was simply, "There is but one God, and Mahomet is His prophet." Still, another cause of Saracen success was the effective plan adopted for the consolidation of their power. In battle they were simply terrible, and the destruction of human life was in some instances without a parallel; yet the widows and children of their fallen foes were universally treated with kindness. As a consequence, the children became ardent disciples of Mahometanism, and the widows often married their former conquerors. This was all the more frequent as polygamy was an established custom. The children of these unions gloried in their descent from their conquering fathers.

No wonder then, that in a little more than a single generation Abderahman wrote to the Caliph that in North Africa and
Andalusia all tribute must cease, as all the children born in
those regions were Mahometans, and Arabic had become the
language of the country.

But above all these causes, the careful student of history will
perceive the hand of Providence. Though Christianity was
paganized, and the priesthood and divine authority were taken
from the earth, God had put forth His hand, and through
agencies the most diverse was disciplining the minds of men
for the reception of truth, and preparing a place and a people
for the coming of the Son of Man.

## CHAPTER IV.

### ACHIEVEMENTS OF THE SARACENS.

INTELLECTUAL STAGNATION—SARACENS AND JEWS REVIVE
LEARNING—UNIVERSITY OF BAGDAD—PUBLIC SCHOOLS—
MEDICAL COLLEGE OF CAIRO—CIRCULATING LIBRARY—
MODERN FORM OF BOOKS—ARABIC NOTATION—DIS-
COVERIES IN CHEMISTRY—ROTUNDITY OF THE EARTH—
MARINER'S COMPASS—DISCOVERIES OF ALHAZIN—ASTRO-
NOMICAL OBSERVATORIES—GOLDEN AGE OF JUDAISM—
CITIES OF ANDALUSIA—SARACEN DWELLINGS—CONDI-
TION OF WOMEN—FEMALE PHYSICIANS.

THE civilized world is dotted over with theological semi-
naries, the teachers in which are considered to be men
well educated in the learning of ancient and modern times.
The avowed purpose of these institutions is to teach the facts,
philosophy and history of the so-called Christian religion, yet
not a teacher in these institutions can be found who dares
to assert the stupendous fact that from the time of the apostles
to the ninth century science, literature and philosophy were
well nigh extinct. During all this time, with the exception

of Jewish and Saracen writers, scarcely a work can be found of sufficient merit to rescue the name of the author from oblivion. Let the skeptic answer this question: Why was it that when the voice of inspiration was hushed and the gospel and its ordinances taken from the earth, there fell upon it an intellectual stagnation, an invisible atmosphere of oppression, ready to crush down morally and physically whatever provoked its weight? Thus the dreary and weary centuries rolled on, until a nation, hitherto considered barbarous, yet of the seed of Abraham, and heirs of the promises made to Ishmael and Esau, aroused society from the hideous fanaticism, ignorance and superstition into which apostasy had plunged it.

If it be true that the Saracens burned the Alexandrian library, it must be considered that this was the act of an uneducated general and the vengeance of the soldiery after a terrible siege, rather than the deliberate policy of the government. Within twenty-five years from the death of Mahomet the Caliphs had become famous for their patronage of learning. Ali, the fourth Caliph and son-in-law of Mahomet, used to say, "The world is sustained by four things only: the prayers of the good, the learning of the wise, the justice of the great, and the valor of the brave." This sentiment was echoed and re-echoed until it became an honored maxim in the minds of millions.

Under the influence of Jewish, Nestorian and Saracen teachers the manners of the Saracens became more polished and their thoughts more elevated. They made conquests in the realms of science, literature and the arts as quickly as in the provinces of the Roman empire.

For example, Almansor, who reigned as Caliph from A. D. 753 to 775, established the University of Bagdad, and endowed it with two hundred thousand pieces of gold, and an annual revenue of fifteen thousand dinars, equal in commercial value to one hundred and twenty thousand dollars of our money. He invited thither learned men from every land, irrespective of their religious opinions. By these men were founded celebrated schools of mathematics, astronomy, chemistry, medicine, law and languages.

His grand-son, Haroun-al-Raschid, ordered in A. D. 786, that a public school should be attached to every mosque in his dominions. This was more than seven hundred years before the establishment of the famous parish schools of Scotland.

The Caliph-al-Mamun, in A. D. 813, founded the great medical college of Cairo, which required students to pass a rigid examination before receiving authority to enter on the practice of their profession. At this college we have the first account of dissecting human bodies for the purpose of ascertaining the nature and locality of diseases, and the first circulating library for students. These books were bound according to the modern form, which then began to be used among the Saracens in place of the ancient form of the scroll.

By the means just mentioned, the ancient sciences were greatly extended and new ones introduced. To the Saracens we are indebted for our present system of arithmetical notation. If, for example, we wish to multiply 1882 by 125 and then attempt it by the ancient method MDCCCLXXXII., multiplied by CXXV., we shall soon perceive the vast superiority of the Arabic system over that formerly in use. No wonder, then that under the ancient system those who were engaged in solving difficult mathematical problems were frequently styled "sweating calculators."

In this case as in many others the Arab has left his impress on this science. For instance, our word cipher, and kindred words, such as decipher, ciphering, etc., are derived from the word *tsaphara*, or *ciphra*, the name for the 0 in the Arabic language.

In experimental sciences, they, originated chemistry and discovered the nature and properties of sulphuric acid, nitric acid, alcohol and many other chemical agents. From their schools of medicine may be traced such words as julep, syrup, elixir, alchemy, etc. To them we are indebted for algebra, or universal arithmetic, and in astronomy they made such advances that many constellations and stars of the first magnitude still retain the Arabic names.

In geography, the Saracens made important discoveries. Hitherto mankind had been taught that the earth was a vast plain, surmounted by an immense vault commonly called the sky. They were the first to prove that the earth is a vast globe, or ball; and in order to determine its size, they first ascertained on the level shore of the Red sea the exact position of the North Star. Then traveling directly north until it had attained another degree of elevation, they measured the distance between these points, and multiplying the result by three hundred and sixty (the number of degrees in a circle), they found the earth to be nearly twenty-five thousand miles in circumference. So accurate were their observations and measurements that the best calculators of recent times differ from them less than one-third of a mile.

Five hundred years later the Roman pontiffs were excommunicating and torturing those who taught the rotundity of the earth. While Catholic monks were teaching, in all its absurdity, the flatness of the earth, and how it rested on a vast rock, and that rock on another and so on all the way down to the bottom(?), the Saracens were teaching geography from globes in their common schools. It cost a long struggle through several centuries, "with spiritual wickedness in high places," before the truth finally triumphed.

European historians have generally given great credit to Pope Gregory for the invention and adoption of the Gregorian calendar and a more accurate method of measuring the exact length of the civil year. Yet, Gregory only adopted what had been discovered and taught by Thebit-Ben-Corrah, the Saracen astronomer, more than five hundred years before, and what Gregory himself had learned in youth while attending a Saracen university.

The mariner's compass was well known to the Arabs, who probably brought it from China and introduced it to the nations of Europe. From this we may correctly infer that they were a maritime people. In fact, long before the time of Mahomet, Arabian merchants were acquainted with the Indies, and even China and the eastern coast of Africa as far south as Madagascar.

Alhazin, who wrote about A. D. 1080, made the great discovery of atmospheric refraction—that a ray of light when it touches the atmosphere is bent from a straight line; and consequently we see the sun before it rises and after it sets, in the same manner that an object lying at the bottom of a bucket filled with water appears in quite a different position from that in which it really is.   He was the first to give that beautiful and scientific explanation of twilight, viz., the refraction of light, which is still regarded by modern scientists as the true one.   He even attempted to ascertain the height of the atmosphere, which he estimated to be about fifty-eight and a half miles.   This philosopher also wrote a treatise on weights and measures, and introduced that excellent system of weighing by means of a small, movable weight attached to the longer arm of a lever, as in our modern scales or steel-yards.   The Arabian astronomer, Ebn-Junis, was the first who made use of the pendulum in the machinery of clocks for the accurate measurement of the hours.

In the golden age of the Saracen empire, there were colleges in every part of its vast dominions.   So numerous were these institutions, that more than six thousand students received instructions in them annually.   In the far east were the college and astronomical observatory of Samercand; while in the western province of Andalusia were the famous school and observatory of Giralda.

The first medical college established in Europe was that founded by the Saracens at Salerno, in Italy; the first famous school of mathematics and astronomy was that established by them at Seville, in Spain.

Among them, learning was not confined to the rich, but every class received its benefits.   The teachers of their colleges were paid liberal salaries for their services, and an allowance was made for indigent scholars, so that the son of the mechanic could graduate from the same class as the heirs of the Caliphs.

At first glance it seems remarkable that the wild ferocity of the Arabs should so suddenly change into a passion for intellectual pursuits; yet it should not be forgotten that this ferocity was to a great extent caused by religious enthusiasm. Thus, when the General Akbah had conquered his way from Egypt to the Atlantic ocean, opposite the Canary Islands, he rode his horse into the sea and drew his sword, exclaiming,

"Great Allah! if my course were not stopped by this sea, I would still go on to the unknown regions of the West, preaching the unity of thy holy name, and putting to the sword the rebellious nations who worship any other gods than thee."

Again, when we consider that a large majority of their teachers and philosophers were of the Jewish nation, we see a beautiful Providence in all this. The remnants of God's chosen people, though exiles and wanderers, despised and down-trodden by the Gentiles, were yet the instruments in God's hands for the execution of His purposes and the elevation of the race.

Surely there is a broader, higher, grander meaning in the promise given to Abraham, "In thy seed shall all the nations of the earth be blessed," than many are willing to admit! And this is all the more remarkable, that, at the very time when mankind so much needed instruction, should occur what Milman so aptly terms, "The golden age of Judaism." Not an age of royal pomp and political power—that passed away with David and Solomon—but an age of intellectual culture, scientific research and practical discovery.

Strange it would appear to the casual student, if upon further research he should find that all great religious teachers have been of Israelitish origin, as well as a large proportion of those who have achieved distinction in the arts and sciences. But it was in Spain, southern France and Sicily that the Saracens attained their greatest power and influence; for there they came in contact with the nations of western Europe, and so influenced European manners, customs and modes of thought that through them that influence has been transmitted to our times.

To the ingenuity of the Saracens we are indebted for the origin of many articles of clothing and personal comfort. Their religion taught them to be clean in person. They did not therefore clothe themselves, according to prevailing customs in that age, in an under-garment made from the skins of wild beasts—a garment which remained unwashed and unchanged until it dropped to pieces of itself, a loathsome mass of vermin, stench and rags. They taught us the use of that often-changed and often-washed garment commonly called a shirt, which still is known among the ladies under its old Arabic name, *chemise*.

To them we are indebted for some of our most valuable fruits, such as the apricot and peach.

Remembering the cooling effects of water in their own hot climate, they spared no pains in constructing artificial lakes and fountains and streams for the irrigation of their gardens.

Andalusia became the paradise of the world. The capital was Cordova, which they greatly embellished as well as the rival cities Toledo, Seville and Granada. A person might walk for miles through their cities after night-fall by the light of their public lamps. Seven hundred years afterwards, not a single public lamp could be found in the city of London. The streets of these cities were solidly paved, through which rolled magnificent carriages, drawn by horses, the fame of which has descended to our times. Five hundred years later the sovereigns of Great Britain and Germany were still traveling in uncouth wagons, drawn by oxen, goaded on by pedestrian drivers.

The sidewalks of Cordova, Toledo, Seville and Granada were paved with flagstones; while at a corresponding period the inhabitant of London or Paris who ventured beyond his threshold on a rainy day sank ankle-deep in filth and mud. Their residences were frequently in the midst of orchards or embosomed in shady groves. They had cool and spacious porches for rest in the heat of the day. Often these porches had roofs of stained glass, on which fell in soothing cadences the glittering pearl-drops of water from elevated fountains.

Their houses were usually built of brick or stone, and contained many apartments, such as sleeping rooms, baths, libraries, parlors and dining halls. In the best class of dwellings, the ceilings were frescoed and the walls covered with paintings, representing scenes of paradise, groves and fruits, lawns and fountains. Yet, delineations of the human form, either nude or partly so, were religiously forbidden, as it was considered that such representations were promotive of licentiousness.

Some of these apartments were furnished with musical instruments, where the young of both sexes were wont to join in mirth and festivity, and dancing to the music of the

INTERIOR OF A SARACEN PALACE.

lute and mandolin. In others, the sedate and reflecting, could engage in scientific research or philosophical discussion. The dwellings of the rich were carpeted, and sometimes warmed by furnaces in winter and cooled in summer with perfumed air, brought by under-ground pipes from distant flower gardens. The use of wine was prohibited. The feasts of the Saracens were marked with sobriety, and furnished a pleasing contrast to the drunken revelries of their northern neighbors.

The enchanting moonlight evenings of Andalusia were frequently spent by the devout in sequestered gardens, consoling themselves for the disappointments of this life by the hope of immortality, and reconciling themselves to their daily toil by the expectation of the joys of paradise, where flowers never fade nor fruits decay, where sickness, and sorrow, and death are known no more.

Under Saracen government, religious persecution was unknown. Students from Great Britain, Ireland, France and Germany came to study at Saracen universities. There, among distinguished characters, whose names and influence have descended to our times, was Frederick, afterwards Frederick II., king of Italy; Gerbert, afterwards famous as Pope Sylvester II.; Peter the Venerable, Abelard, the poet, and Arnold of Brescia.

No wonder then that the Saracens looked with contempt upon the barbarism of the native races of Europe, who could scarcely be said to have emerged from the savage state—unclean in person, benighted in mind, inhabiting huts in which it was a mark of wealth if there were bulrushes on the floor and straw mats against the wall; subsisting on barley, beans, cabbages, herbs and even the bark of trees; clothed in rudely-tanned skins of wild animals, which were famous indeed for durability, but not very conducive to personal cleanliness.

But the arts, sciences and general culture were not confined to the Saracen men alone. Among the women there were many who, like Valada, Ayesha, Labana and Algasania, achieved a national reputation. Some of these were daughters of Caliphs, who considered it not beneath their dignity to devote their lives to science and the elevation of their sex. Where shall we find their equals at that time in so-called Christian countries? Albucasis, a celebrated physician of Cordova, in his medical works, makes mention of several female physicians, and recommends the employment of such in certain cases. No doubt the condition of women was superior and their duties and position better understood among polygamous Saracens than in monogamous Christendom.

The foregoing will indicate to some extent the condition of Saracen society in the tenth and eleventh centuries. Shall we compare it with the contemporary barbarism of the other portions of Europe?

Were we to pursue this subject further it would not be difficult to show that Venice owed her commercial greatness to Saracen fleets and Jewish merchants; that Marco Polo only traveled over countries already well delineated on maps, and well described by Abulfeda and other Arabian geographers; that, Columbus himself first received scientific proof of the rotundity of the earth while corresponding with Torricelli, the great Florentine astronomer, who in turn had received his education at the Saracen university of Seville, and modelled his globes, maps and charts from those in its possession.

The careful student of history must deplore the attempts made by many historians to ignore our indebtedness to the Saracens, who in the providence of God have left their impress on the religions, arts and sciences of the world. Surely prejudice founded on national conceit and sectarian bigotry cannot last forever.

# CHAPTER V.

## REMARKABLE CITIES OF MEDIEVAL TIMES.

JERUSALEM THE SACRED CITY—ALEXANDRIA NOTED FOR
PHILOSOPHY—SCHOOL OF HYPATIA—MOB MURDERS HER
—DOCTRINES OF CYRIL—JERUSALEM A SCENE OF SUFFER-
ING—FULFILLMENT OF PROPHECY—HERCULANEUM AND
POMPEII—THEIR DESTRUCTION—EVIDENCES OF THEIR
WICKEDNESS—EXCAVATIONS—ROMAN RULE—REMOVAL
OF CAPITAL—CRIMES OF CONSTANTINE—COMMENCEMENT
OF GREEK EMPIRE—DESCRIPTION OF CONSTANTINOPLE
—ITS CAPTURE BY CRUSADERS—TAKEN BY THE TURKS—
INTELLECTUAL DEGRADATION—PRIESTCRAFT—DEBAUCH-
ERY—TURKISH RULE.

THE four great cities of medieval times were Jerusalem, Rome, Alexandria and Constantinople. The first named has ever been the sacred city, not merely of the Jews, but also of devout Christian pilgrims of all ages. During the crusades it was the great object for the possession of which so much blood and treasure were expended.

Alexandria, for the first three centuries of the Christian era, was the commercial metropolis of the world, as well as the chief seat of pagan learning and philosophy. It was here that Hypatia, the daughter of Theon, the mathematician, held her famous school. Each day before her academy stood a long train of chariots. Her lecture room was crowded with the cultured classes of Alexandria. They came to ask those profound questions that human reason, unaided, can never answer: "What am I? Where am I? What can I know?"

At this time, Cyril, archbishop of Alexandria, was attempting to force upon the world his trinitarian views. His absurd ideas could not endure the sharp criticism of philosophic minds. Cyril employed a mob of Alexandrian monks. Amid the fearful yelling of these bare-legged and black-cowled fiends, Hypatia was dragged from her chariot. In mortal terror she fled to an adjacent church, and was there brutally murdered by the club of Peter the Reader. But this was not all. We can only get a faint idea of the depraved condition of paganized Christianity, when we call to mind the fact that the monks finished their infernal crime by dismembering her body and scraping the flesh from her bones with oyster shells.

Cyril then procured the banishment of all who held opposing doctrines, and thus his absurd doctrines were forced upon society. Such was the debased condition of society in a city where had been planted one of the apostolic churches. As vice increased her prosperity decreased. During the reign of Constantine, the influence of Alexandria was much diminished, and with the Mahometan conquest it fell to the rank of a provincial town.

Jerusalem, once the "glory of the earth, and the pride of the nations," never recovered from the siege by Titus, in A. D. 70. The answer which the Jews made to Pilate, "*His blood be upon us and upon our children*," which they spake in reference to the Savior, has been terribly and literally fulfilled. It may be safely asserted that Jerusalem has witnessed more scenes of human suffering than any other spot on earth.

Who does not see the hand of Providence in her retribution, as well as in the fate of Herculaneum and Pompeii?

These cities were destroyed in A. D. 79, by an eruption of Mount Vesuvius, and buried by a shower of ashes, sand and stones. Herculaneum was situated about eight miles south of the present city of Naples, and Pompeii about fifteen miles eastward.

Thus they remained buried for nearly seventeen hundred years. Extensive excavations have been made during the past century, disclosing the city walls, streets, temples, theatres, private dwellings, domestic utensils and statuary. Many objects have been found which indicate the wicked and licentious character of the inhabitants, and go to prove that they were ripe for the destruction which awaited them. The inhabitants died just as the catastrophe found them, guests in their banqueting halls, soldiers at their posts, prisoners in their dungeons, maidens at the mirror and students at their books.

ERUPTION OF MOUNT VESUVIUS.

When the city was unearthed, the houses were found standing. The interior paintings were still fresh, and the skeletons remained in the very position and the very place in which death had overtaken them so long ago. The marks left by the cups of the tiplers still remained on the counters; the prisoners still wore their fetters, the ladies their chains and bracelets. The researches are still going on, new wonders are every day coming to light, and we shall soon have quite a distinct idea of Roman towns in the first century of the Christian era.

Rome, from before the commencement of the Christian era, had been the political and military capital of the world. From her gates issued forth those imperial armies that conquered nations and crushed the liberties of mankind. Her rule was not one of reason but one of force. From the age of Augustus Cæsar her power had been waning, and when the Emperor Constantine removed the capital to Constantinople, Rome became a city of secondary importance. Though her political prestige was gone she became the seat of a religious empire which had and still has a mighty influence in the nations of the earth. The wrongs which she inflicted on others have recoiled with terrible retribution on herself. Her ruins are silent and majestic witnesses of the providence of God.

To the reign of Constantine the Great, must be referred the commencement of those dark and dismal times which oppressed Europe for a thousand years.

Constantine, while dwelling at Rome, had murdered his son Crispus, his nephew Licinius, and had suffocated, in a steam bath, his wife, Fausta, to whom he had been married twenty years, and who was the mother of three of his sons.

The public abhorance of his crimes could no longer be concealed. Constantine therefore determined to change his residence and build another metropolis, which he named in honor of himself. He also found it politic to favor the paganized and wrangling Christian sects, that by their aid he might be able to triumph over the powerful coalition that had been formed against him. The reign of Constantine is therefore the true close of the Roman empire: the beginning of the Greek. The transition from the one to the other is emphatically and abruptly marked, by a new metropolis and a new national religion.

Constantinople, at present the capital of the Turkish empire, stands, like Rome, on seven hills, and on a tongue of land projecting into the Bosphorus, which here forms an inlet or small bay known as the Golden Horn.

The Bosphorus, as most of our readers are aware, is the name given to the strait through which flow the waters of the Black sea into the sea of Marmora, and which divides Europe from Asia.

Constantinople is admirably situated for commerce. This is one reason why Russia has so long looked upon it with a covetous eye. In fact, the reason why the bay, on the shores of which the city is built, has been called the "Golden Horn," or horn of abundance, is because into it was brought the wealth of three continents and the products of every clime.

That which is commonly called Constantinople, in reality consists of three great cities, divided by arms of the sea, yet so near to each other that the edifices of either of the cities may be seen distinctly from the other two.

The view here given represents Constantinople looking from the north. In the background is seen the city of Scutari, on the Asiatic side of the Bosphorus. The hills in the distance are those of Asia Minor. On the right is shown the city of Stamboul, which stands on the site of the ancient Byzantium, and the foreground represents the modern city of Galata, where the greater part of the foreign population resides, and where the exchange, custom-house, and most of the churches, convents and hospitals are situated.

As here depicted the current of the Bosphorus flows from left to right and disappears in the distance.

The history of this city is very remarkable, and runs far back into the mist of antiquity. Long before the Christian era it was a place of considerable trade and political importance. Here the barbarians from the coast of the Black sea came to barter their furs for the products of more favored regions. Near this point Alexander the Great crossed the Bosphorus on his great campaign of eastern conquest. In the second century before Christ, the Romans having subdued the neighboring

countries, built a fort on the site of the ancient city and named it Byzantium.

The Roman emperor, Constantine the Great, enlarged and beautified the city and made it the capital of the Roman empire, and in honor of himself changed the name to Constantinople.    After his death the Roman empire was divided, and Constantinople continued to be the capital of the eastern division.

For more than one thousand years it was the residence of the Cæsars and the commercial metropolis of the world.

Owing to the religious rivalry of Rome it was taken and partly burned, by the Crusaders, in A. D. 1205.    But the most memorable siege it has ever endured was in A. D. 1453, when it fell into the hands of the Ottoman Turks.    By a strange coincidence a Constantine gave his name to the city, and a Constantine reigned at its fall.

It was on the morning of April 6th, A. D. 1453, that Mahomet II., gave the signal for the attack, and the Turkish cannon (then a new invention) thundered against the walls of the city.    For fifty days the siege was carried on with little success. At last, food was getting scarce, and the pangs of hunger were sorely felt by the Christians within the city.    But hope revived as away on the sea of Marmora, they spied five great ships well laden with supplies and with the Christian flag unfurled. Onward the vessels flew before the breeze, but what a sight met them as they neared the port!    Three hundred Turkish ships were drawn up in a line across the straits, each filled with troops and eager for the fight.    But there were brave hearts in those five gallant Christian ships, full willing to meet the outnumbering enemy.    Gaily they careened before the swelling breeze, and steering straight for the Turkish line bore down upon the foe.    Suddenly from the Christian ranks there burst a joyous shout, as the Turkish ships first wavered and then fled.    In vain the fierce sultan, Mahomet II., mad with rage, called upon his captains to make good the fight. But the rent was made, and amid a hundred thousand Christian cheers the succoring ships sailed in victoriously to the Golden Horn, and many a mother's heart was glad as she closely clasped her half-famished child.

A strong chain had meanwhile been placed across the harbor, to prevent the entrance of the Turkish fleet. But Mahomet was determined not to be baffled. In the silence of the night he caused eighty boats to be dragged ten miles across the neck of land that divides the sea of Marmora from the tip of the Golden Horn. Rafts were then made, on which cannon were floated to bombard the city from the harbor.

By the 29th of May all was ready for the final battle. The great Byzantine empire, once foremost in the powers of the world, had shrunk into the narrow limits of a few square miles.

The sun had set, and night fell upon the contending hosts. Christian warriors, as they lay under the starry canopy of heaven, cast off the sterner half of man, and let their softer natures free: and loving thoughts of sisters, mothers, wives went winding through the air, to meet in last embrace.

And now the solemn calm before the storm drew near, and all was hushed and still. Constantine did not sleep. He knew that his hour was at hand. With a few chosen knights, he retired to the great church of St. Sophia, and there uncovered stood before the cross. To-morrow the great Byzantine empire would pass away with him! His tears fell thickly at the thought; and he prayed that he might die as became a Christian knight. Then for the last time he partook of the sacrament, and, turning to those around, he said, "I pray forgiveness if I have injured any one in thought, or word, or deed."

He stepped to the portal of the church, where stood his impatient steed, placed his helmet on his noble head, and mounting into the saddle, the humble penitent rode off as warrior Christian king, to battle and to die. He was afterwards found among a heap of the slain.

The banner of the cresent waved over the waters of the Bosphorus, and what was then the richest capital and finest country in Europe. Four hundred and thirty years have rolled by since then. It is still in their possession.

The appearance of Constantinople at the present time is very peculiar. The city is embosomed in gardens, orchards and vineyards. The houses are for the most part built in the form of a hollow square, with flat roofs and the windows facing inward. This gives to the compact parts of the city a rather dingy appearance. The streets, especially in the ancient portions, are extremely narrow, and frequently filthy. It is therefore pleasant to turn from these crowded thoroughfares, and in a few moments' walk, find yourself surrounded with shady trees, singing birds, fountains and flowers.

Here, in the limits of a single city, may be found representatives of almost every race and clime. The fair-haired natives of northern Europe, the swarthy inhabitants of Tartary, tall fierce-looking Circassians, and flat-nosed, woolly-headed negroes from central Africa; all mingling with the more polished inhabitants of western Europe, each dressed in his own peculiar garb, and presenting a living picture no less striking than strange. In this great hive of humanity may be heard at least fifty different languages making a complete Babel of sounds. Here, also, may be seen in striking contrast, the different manners, customs and usages of oriental and western nations.

The different methods used in the transportation of merchandise are no less peculiar; for while on the eastern side of the city, may be seen approaching long caravans of camels laden with the rich products of the East, on the western side may be heard the shriek of the locomotive, announcing the arrival of a train, bringing passengers, merchandise and latest intelligence from western nations.

But the most significant custom is that five times a day the *muezzins*, or Mahometan priests, ascend to the top of the mosques (as places of worship are called) and which are thickly scattered through the city, and in a loud wailing voice exclaim, "God is great! There is one God! Mahomet is His prophet! Come to prayer!" This is repeated four times facing the east, south, west and north, and has a penetrating effect on the mind of the hearer, much more than the sound of the church-bell of the Christians, or the trumpet of the Jews.

Most European historians have lamented the seizure of Constantinople by the Turks as a terrible disaster. To the unprejudiced student of history there seems to be but little reason for regret. For eleven hundred years Constantinople had greatly influenced the destinies of the world; but during all that time her power had tended more to the degradation than to the elevation of mankind. Her citizens possessed all the classical writings and works of art of the great authors of antiquity; yet in a thousand years they never produced one original, never advanced one step in philosophy or science, or made a single practical discovery. What was it that produced this barrenness, this intellectual degradation in Constantinople? It was the tyranny of priestcraft over thought. For a thousand years Constantinople had been not merely the leading commercial city, but also the leading city in debauchery and crime. In this respect it has vastly improved under Turkish rule. At the present time, especially in the Mahometan portions of the city, it is the least licentious of all the great capitals of modern Europe.

# CHAPTER VI.

## RELIC-WORSHIP, PILGRIMAGES AND CRUSADES.

GROWTH OF RELIC-WORSHIP—SCHEMES OF THE ROMAN PONTIFFS—MANUFACTURE OF RELICS—THEIR GREAT VARIETY—VALUE OF RELICS—INSULTS OFFERED TO PILGRIMS—PETER THE HERMIT—CRUSADES—DISORDERLY RABBLE—TERRIBLE SUFFERING—CAPTURE OF JERUSALEM —TERRIBLE MASSACRE—CAPTURE OF CONSTANTINOPLE— CRUSADES OF THE CHILDREN—RESULT OF THE CRUSADES —REVIVAL OF LEARNING.

IN previous chapters has been traced the apostasy of the early church, also the career of Mahomet, and the conquests and achievements of the Saracens. While these events were transpiring, other causes were at work which led eventually to the elevation of mankind, the history of which plainly indicates the workings of an All-wise Providence.

At this period there were no printed books, and the only means of religious instruction to which the masses had access, were the pictures and images to be found in the churches, together with the explanations of them given by the priests. By means of these practical object-lessons much useful information was imparted. The principal events in the life of our Savior were thus depicted, and, though the people did not fully understand the grandeur of His mission, they at least learned something of His history, their duties to each other and their own future destiny.

Thus there came to be associated in their minds a reverence for the picture or image itself, and this idea extended until it included the localities where the great events of the Savior's life, death and resurrection transpired.

With the growth of devotion to the person of Christ, grew the feeling of reverence for every place which He had visited and every memorial which He had left behind Him. The impulse once given, soon became irresistible. Every incident of the gospel narratives was associated with some particular spot, and millions believed that the sight of these places brought them nearer to heaven. The cave or excavation in which it was said the Redeemer was born, and where the wise men of the East laid before Him their royal gifts of gold, frankincense and myrrh, the mount from which He uttered His blessings on the meek, the merciful and the pure in heart, in short, every spot connected with his life, death and resurrection called forth emotions of passionate veneration. These feelings were greatly intensified by the alleged discovery of the cross on which the Savior died, together with the two crosses on which the thieves were crucified.

The splendid churches raised by the Emperor Constantine and his mother Helena over the supposed spot of our Savior's birth at Bethlehem, and His sepulchre at Jerusalem, became for the Christian of that day what the tomb of the prophet at Medina became afterwards to the followers of Mahomet.

The remission of sins and eternal rewards in the world to come were the blessings promised to the weary pilgrim when he should tread the classic soil of Judea, bathe in the river Jordan, chant his quiet anthem of praise in the cave at Bethlehem, walk in the quiet shades of Gethsemane and kneel in reverence at the Savior's tomb.

No wonder 'then that a hundred thousand pilgrims might have been seen each year wending their way across the plains of Asia Minor, destined for Jerusalem.

The Roman pontiffs, owing to the ignorance of the times, had already built up a wide-spread system of superstition.

CHURCH OF THE HOLY SEPULCHRE.

They held almost imperial sway over the countless hordes of central and northern Europe. Even kings and emperors paid tribute, and sovereigns dared not disobey their commands. As an instance, might be mentioned Henry IV., of Germany, who having displeased Pope Gregory VII., was obliged, under penalty of losing his kingdom, to stand as a penitent at the pope's castle gate during three dreary winter

days, seeking pardon and reconciliation of the inexorable
pontiff.

It is not surprising that the popes, who had long trafficked
in human credulity, saw, in the growth of relic-worship, an
opportunity to increase their own power and the revenues of
the church of Rome.    Accordingly an understanding was
made with the monks of Palestine and relics were manu-
factured in untold numbers.

An amusing and instructive chapter might be written on
this subject: amusing because of its absurdity, and instructive
as it shows to what extremes of folly men will go when left
without the guidance of the Holy Spirit.

The crimes and corruptions of the papacy had destroyed public confidence.    The devout instinctively turned with reverence
towards every object that recalled the memories of the pure
and good who once lived upon the earth.

No sooner had the wild rage for relics fairly set in than each
monastery in the vicinity of Jerusalem made a specialty of
some particular relic.    The monks at Bethlehem sold thousands
of pounds of half rotten rags, each fragment purporting
to be a portion of the swaddling cloths of the infant
Savior.    The monks who guarded the supposed sepulchre of
Christ, sold hundreds of thousands of little chips of stone
said to have been broken off from the very walls of the tomb
where the body of Jesus had lain.    It does not seem to have
shaken the credulity of the pilgrims in the least, that the
tomb still remained in as good repair as ever, and showed no
marks of demolition.

The monks who inhabited the monasteries on the banks of
the Jordan could point to at least twenty places where it was
said the Savior had been baptized, and each monastery
possessed numerous pebbles which the monks claimed had
been touched by His feet.    No less than seven monasteries
claimed to have the true cross in their possession, and thousands of pieces, of wood amounting to many tons in weight,
were sold to devout pilgrims.    Each of these pieces, it was
claimed, was a part of the true cross.

But it would require a long and tedious list to even enumer-
ate the various articles comprised in this relic-worship.    In

order to get some faint idea of their extent and variety, the relics which the Abbot Martin obtained for his monastery in Alsace might be mentioned.   These, among other things, included "a piece of the true cross, a fragment of the infant Savior's swaddling cloths, some pebbles from the river Jordan which the Savior's feet had touched, a branch of the tree under which He prayed in the garden of Gethsemane, a piece of the Savior's robe, for which the Roman soldiers cast lots," (see Matthew, 27th chapter), "a tooth of St. Mark, seven hairs of the martyr, Stephen, a thigh bone of the animal which Jesus rode into Jerusalem," (see Luke, 19th chapter), and (I hesitate to write such blasphemy) "a bottle of the milk of the mother of God."

In connection with this relic-worship, an amusing anecdote is related: It so happened that about thirty pilgrims were traveling homeward from Palestine together.   Being somewhat weary, they concluded to rest and refresh themselves. Having partaken of some wine too freely they commenced to boast of the various relics which each had in his possession. One claimed that he had actually the identical piece of money which Peter took out of the fish's mouth (see Matthew, 17th chapter, 27th verse).   But, to their mutual surprise, they soon found that each had made a similar purchase.   It was plain that at least twenty-nine of them had been defrauded.   But they reasoned that if it was not wrong for the monks to defraud them, it would not be wrong for them to defraud others.   So they quietly sold the pieces of money as soon as possible.

No doubt one reason why relic-worship became so extensive, was the encouragement given to it by the Roman pontiffs.   It was boldly asserted that the possession of a relic was a specific against evil spirits, accidents, disease, and, in short, nearly every evil to which humanity is heir.   Hence the great demand for relics by the ignorant and superstitious, and the vast sums of money which were thus poured into the treasury of the church of Rome.

For example, a tooth of an apostle was valued at a sum equal commercially to one hundred dollars of our money, and a thousand dollars would scarcely buy a piece of the true cross

3

as large as a common friction match.   Of course these prices
varied according to the wealth and the credulity of the pur-
chaser.

When, in A. D. 637, Jerusalem was captured by the Saracens, the Christians and pilgrims were treated with much consideration.    They were not only to be safe in their persons,
but undisturbed in the exercise of their religion and in the use
of their churches.

The yearly influx of at least one hundred thousand pilgrims,
however, aroused suspicion among the great mass of Mahometans, who failed to comprehend the purport of their extraordinary journey, but perceived the necessity of putting some
restraint on this annual rush of such countless multitudes.
The consequence was that wrongs were inflicted and retaliated
until the mere journey to Jerusalem involved dangers from
which even the bravest might shrink.    Insults offered to the
pilgrims were accompanied by insults offered to the holy places
and to those who ministered in them.

Still the pilgrims went forth by thousands, and occasionally
hundreds and frequently only tens returned to recount the
miseries and wanton cruelties they had undergone.

Throughout the length and breadth of Christendom a
fierce indignation was stirring the hearts of men, and their rage,
like pent up waters, needed only an opportunity to rush forth
as a flood over the lands under the control of the Mahometans.    That opportunity was not long wanting.    Peter, the
hermit, who had witnessed the barbarities to which the
pilgrims were exposed, roused Europe to a frantic state by his
preaching.

Dwarfish in stature and mean in person, he was yet filled
with a zeal that knew no bounds.    The horrors which fired
his soul were those which would most surely stir the conscience
and arouse the wrath of his hearers.    His fiery appeals carried
everything before him.    Wherever he went, the rich and the
poor, the aged and the young, the nobles and the peasants
thronged in thousands around the emaciated stranger.    He
traveled with his head and feet bare, calling on all classes to
deliver from the unbeliever the land which was the cradle of
their faith.

The vehemence which choked his own utterance became contagious. His sobs and groans called forth the tears and cries of the vast crowds who hung upon his words and greedily devoured the harrowing accounts of the pilgrims, whom Peter brought forward as witnesses of the truth of his picture. The excitement and frenzy of the moment threw, no doubt, a specious coloring, over an enterprise of doubtful morality, and which eventually pandered to the basest passion of humanity.

These wars are known in history by the name of Crusades, from the Latin term *crux*, a cross, which emblem was painted on the breasts or shoulders of all who engaged in them.

When the masses were thoroughly excited, Pope Urban gave the enterprise his sanction, and promised to all who would enlist a full remission of their sins. This encouraged innumerable desperadoes to assume the badge of the cross. Fanaticism and hypocrisy, lust and avarice strangely urged their several votaries to pursue one path, and all under the sacred and now woefully profaned name of Christian zeal!

Yet the hand of Providence was in all this. Even the rage of men worked out His purpose, and, as the sequel will show, produced results which, under the controlling hand of God led to the elevation of the race.

To give a detailed description of the Crusades would alone require a volume. It is enough to say that the first Crusade failed, not only disastrously, but hideously, so far as the ignorant rabbles under Peter, the hermit, and Walter, the penniless, were concerned. The long and ghastly line of bones whitening the roadside all the way from Hungary to Judea, showed how different a thing it was for a peaceable and solitary pilgrim with his staff and wallet and scallop-shell to beg his way, and the disorderly rabble of thousands upon thousands to rush forward without any organization, and gathering their daily supplies by robbing and killing the helpless peasants on their route. This, in their ignorance or blasphemy, they called "trusting in the providence of God."

The van of the Crusades consisted of two hundred and seventy-five thousand men. Behind these came a rabble of

two hundred thousand men, women and children, preceded
by a goat and a goose, into which some blasphemous lunatic
had told them that the Holy Ghost had entered. When at
length these animals died, a representation of them was painted
on their banner.

In this vile horde no pretense was kept up of order or of
decency. Driven to madness by disappointment and famine,
and expecting, in their ignorance, that every town they came
to must be Jerusalem, they laid hands on whatever they could
in their extremity. Their track was marked by robbery, fire
and bloodshed. In the first Crusade alone, more than five
hundred thousand human beings perished. However, a
better organized expedition soon followed, commanded by
Godfrey de Bouillon, Duke of Lorraine. By him Jerusalem
was captured July 15th, A. D. 1099. As might be expected,
its siege and capture were attended by the perpetration of
cruelties almost surpassing belief.

What a contrast to the conduct of the Arabs, when the
Caliph Omar took Jerusalem, A. D. 637! He rode into the city
by the side of the patriarch, Saphronius, conversing with him
on its antiquities. When the time of evening prayer arrived,
he declined to pay his devotions in the church of Constantine,
fearing that his followers might wish to imitate his example,
and thus render it practically useless to the Christians; but he
knelt outside in the yard near the entrance gate. What a supreme
act of religious toleration! When will free-born Americans
learn to act thus nobly?

But in the capture of Jerusalem by the Crusaders the
brains of young children were dashed out against the walls,
infants were thrown over the battlements, men and women
were tortured that they might be compelled to disclose hidden
wealth, the Jews were driven into their synagogue and there
burnt. A massacre of seventy thousand persons took place, and
the pope's especial ambassador was seen "partaking in the
triumph."

Such were the exploits of the first Crusade. The second
was barren of results except the inhuman butchery of thousands of unoffending Jews. The third produced no permanent
effects, but a halo of false glory is shed around it, from the

exploits of Richard the Lion-heart, king of England, who was connected with it, and whose adventures have stirred to enthusiasm even the dullest of historians. With great difficulty, Pope Innocent III., succeeded in preparing the fourth Crusade, A. D. 1202. The government of Venice agreed to furnish ships to carry them to Palestine, but, actuated·by a love of plunder, and a desire to gratify the bitter feeling which existed between the popes of Rome and the bishops of Constantinople, they turned aside to vent their rage on their fellow-Christians. Constantinople was taken by storm A. D. 1204. On the night of its capture more houses were burned than could be found in any three of the largest cities of France. The treasures of the churches were carried away, and even the tombs of the ancient emperors were rifled in the mad search for relics.

Thus, Crusade followed Crusade for more than one hundred and fifty years, until nine armies, comprising more than three millions of men, laid their bodies down to decay and their bones to whiten on the plains and hill-sides of the East.

Among all the enterpises, none were more wild and wicked than those which are called the "Crusades of the children." Emissaries from Rome went throughout Western Europe, preaching and declaring that God would only give the Holy Land into the hands of innocent children. Pope Innocent III. applauded their wild enthusiasm. "These children," said he, "are a reproach to us of riper age. While they hurry to Palestine, we are asleep."

A few words will suffice to tell the story how twenty thousand children, under the boy Stephen, encamped around Vendome. In less than a month ten thousand of them had perished or strayed away. When they reached Marseilles, they lingered near the shore, expecting the Mediterranean to divide, and, like the Red Sea in ancient times, give them a dry passage to Palestine. At length two merchants offered to convey them there in ships, without charge; but at the end of their journey they found themselves, not in Palestine, but in the slave markets of Alexandria and Algiers.

A sequel to this "o'er true tale" is found in the sufferings of another rabble of thirty thousand boys and girls, who, under

ANCIENT VESSELS.

the peasant lad, Nicholas, in crossing the Alps lost nearly half their number. Five thousand reached Genoa, and, being invited by the senate, concluded to settle there. The rest marched to Brindisi, and, setting sail for Palestine, were never heard of more.

Worthless in themselves and wholly useless as a means for founding any permanent dominion in Palestine or elsewhere, these enterprises were a means in the overruling hand of God of effecting the nations of Europe in a way which the promoters never dreamed of.

Their results were many and various. One was that they drew away many of the warlike and turbulent, and gave, as it were, a resting time for the states of Western Europe, during which, learning, science and general culture, among the quietly-disposed, made rapid advances, and many cities and smaller states rose from obscurity to opulence and power.

Another was the change of feeling which took place in the Crusaders themselves. What a surprise awaited these religious barbarians—for such they really were—when for the first time they gazed on the splendors of Constantinople in its palmiest days! What a contrast to their own rude homes, when they passed into Asia Minor, that garden of the world, presenting well-cultivated fields, orchards, vineyards, palaces and schools, the civilization of a thousand years! How unexpected the character of those Saracens, whom they had been taught to regard as no better than bloodthirsty fiends, but whom they found to be valiant, merciful and just!

When Richard the Lion-heart, king of England, lay in his tent consumed by a fever, there came into the camp camels laden with snow, from Mount Lebanon, to assuage his disease. It was a present from his enemy, the great Mahometan Saladin —the homage of one brave soldier to another. But when Richard was returning to England it was by a Christian prince, who should have aided him, that he was treacherously seized and secretly confined.

This was doubtless only one of many such incidents. Every Crusader must have recognized the difference between what they had anticipated and what they had found. They had seen undaunted courage, chivalrous bearing, intellectual culture and

religious toleration far greater than their own.    When the
Crusaders returned to their native lands, they carried with them
the memory of their experiences, and a relish for more polished
manners and a higher civilization than that to which they had
been accustomed at home.    Hence, immediately after the
Crusades the arts and sciences began to be sedulously cultivated
in Europe.    They had departed with the intent of conquering,
aye even exterminating their enemies; but by contact with
those enemies they had learned in some things "a more excellent way."    The words of the Koran inscribed on the banner
of Saladin are true:    "There is no conqueror but God!"
Equally true the words written by the Prophet Esdras, as he
sat by the side of the willow-fringed river of Babylon more
than twenty-three hundred years ago:    "As for truth, it
endureth and is always strong; it liveth and conquereth for
evermore," (see Apocrypha, I. Esdras, iv., 38).

## CHAPTER VII.

### THE DAWN OF MODERN INTELLIGENCE.

THE MORNING DAWNS—RISE OF KNIGHTHOOD—PRINCIPLES
OF KNIGHTS—APOSTATE PRIESTS HELD IN CONTEMPT—
WALDENSES—PERSECUTIONS IN SOUTHERN FRANCE—
RISE OF THE INQUISITION—LIBERAL POLICY OF FREDERICK
—"EVERLASTING GOSPEL"—ITS REMARKABLE TEACH-
INGS—BACON'S DISCOVERIES—GEOGRAPHICAL KNOWL-
EDGE—AZORES AND CANARY ISLANDS—TRAVELS OF
MARCO POLO—CONDITION OF EUROPEAN STATES—
MODERN STATES.

THOSE who have waited for the dawning of the morning
in the latter part of a clear summer night, can understand
the delight experienced at the first tokens of approaching day.
At first the rays of light are very faint and only perceptible to
a keen and experienced eye.    As time wears on the timid
approach of twilight becomes more perceptible.    The intense
blue of the sky begins to soften.    The rays that first darted up

in the far north-east, though occasionally intercepted by mountains or banks of clouds, gradually swing around to the east. The darkness of the night dissolves into the glories of the dawn. The great watch-stars fade away, one by one. The whole firmament is filled with the inflowing tides of morning light. At length a stream of golden sunlight flashes out from above the hills and turns the dewy tear-drops of flower and leaf into rubies and diamonds. Thus the king of day begins his course arrayed in glories too severe for the gaze of man.

In like manner we may in imagination gaze at the dawning of "the dispensation of the fullness of times," and watch the increasing rays of moral, intellectual and spiritual light, feeble indeed at first, yet constantly growing stronger, though sometimes intercepted by mountains of bigotry and mists of error, until at length the gospel's glorious sunshine again lights a benighted world, and the divine authority and Priesthood are restored to the children of men. But let us not anticipate. Let us rather patiently decipher on history's scroll the characters written there by the finger of God. Let us carefully watch the development of His purposes amid the strife and commotion of those perilous times.

With the close of the Crusades the midnight darkness of human history ended. Human misery had reached its climax. Superstition and ignorance had done their most terrible work. Thousands, aye even millions had had an opportunity of comparing the teachings and pretenses of Rome with other civilizations. It is almost needless to say that Catholicism had seriously suffered by the comparison. Rome was weighed in the balance and found wanting.

Those of the Crusaders who remained in Palestine were soon blended with the Mahometan population, and in a few years scarce a vestige of them remained. Many of the leaders who returned were, like Richard the Lion-Hearted, full of praise of the treatment they had received from their enemies, and spent much of their time in founding various orders of chivalry and knighthood. At first those orders received the benediction of the popes. Some of them were even organized before they returned from the Holy Land. Of such were the famous

knights of St. John and Knights Hospitaller. But it was soon
found that those brave men loved liberty more than priestcraft,
so after a time, notwithstanding their eminent services, they
were weakened and divided by stratagem, charges were preferred against them and they were cruelly put to death. The
story of their fate will ever remain one of the darkest pages in
the annals of our race. But their death only accellerated the
progress of their ideas. The spirit and institutions of chivalry
spread rapidly.

Treachery and hypocrisy were held by them in detestation.
"To speak the truth, to succor the helpless and never turn back
from an enemy," was the first vow of the youth who sought
the honors of chivalry.

In an age of darkness and degradation, chivalry developed the
character of woman. It caused her virtues to be appreciated
and honored, made her the equal and companion of man, and
the object of his love and devotion. The love of God and the
protection of women were enjoined as a single duty (see
Halem's Middle Ages, page 512). He who was faithful to his
vow and true to his wife was sure of salvation in the opinion of
the knights, though he failed to perform the penance prescribed
by the Romish clergy.

Chivalry was the religion of the heart, in a rude and untu-
tored age. It had the effect of infusing more of humanity
and generous principle into the operations of war than the
ancient nations had any conception of. Hence we seldom or
never hear in modern times of such scenes of unmingled
atrocity, such deadly treachery, such extensive and cold-blooded
massacres as we so frequently read of in ancient pagan or papal
history.

At the close of the Crusades a great change commenced in
society. The minstrels, who with harps had gone about singing ballads, commemorating deeds of heroism and adventure,
now changed their theme and sang songs of a very different
character. Amid shouts of laughter they went through the
land, wagging their heads, and slyly winking their eyes, and
singing derisive songs about the amours of the priests, who in
turn were not slow to denounce the minstrels as lewd blas-
phemers and atheists.

While the young were singing, the old were thinking; while the gay were carried away with romance and chivalry, the grave and reflecting were falling into heresy.

About A. D. 1100, Peter Waldo, a wealthy citizen of Lyons, became convinced of the corruptions of Rome. He, probably aided by others, translated the scriptures into Provencal French. Thus, to him the world is indebted for the first translation of the Bible into a modern tongue. Waldo could not long remain in Lyons. He fled into Germany and afterwards settled in Bohemia, where he died about A. D. 1179. He was the instrument of spreading those liberal ideas in Bohemia, of which John Huss and Jerome of Prague became in after times worthy representatives. At the time of his death it is said that Waldo had five hundred thousand followers.

Already, A. D. 1134, Peter de Brueys had been burned at Languedoc for denying infant baptism. Already the valleys of Piedmont were full of Waldenses, who denounced the greed of the popes and the intermingling of bishops in bloodshed and war. At this juncture Innocent III., ascended the pontifical throne. Here was a state of things which, as he considered, demanded immediate attention. The methods to which he resorted for the suppression and extinction of heretics, as misbelievers were called, have made his name forever infamous.

Innocent well knew that the greed and the corruptions of the clergy had made them unpopular with the people. He therefore established the mendicant orders of priests, more commonly known under the names of Franciscans and Dominicans. Vowed to poverty and living on alms, they lived and moved among the masses, and yet were held sacred. The accusations and dissipation of luxury so forcibly urged against the regular clergy, were altogether inapplicable to these half-starved wandering fanatics. Once more for a time the popes had gained possession of the ear of the masses.

At this time Southern France was the garden of reform. Here the eloquence of Abelard, the patriotism of Arnold and the statesmanship of Frederick wielded a mighty influence. Like seeds falling into good ground, they brought forth much fruit. Already Arnold had been burned at the stake and his

ashes thrown on the waves of the Tiber.   He has thus become
the heritage, as it were, of every nation  whose shores are
washed by the tides of the sea.   Seven centuries have rolled
by since then, yet the memory of Arnold of Brescia is
ever green; the principles for which he lived and died are
now incorporated in every constitutional government on the
globe.

In no land were his principles more prevalent than in
Southern France, and on it Innocent determined to vent his
rage.  In looking around for a suitable pretext that would rouse
the masses and excite them to religious frenzy, he soon discovered the object for which he sought.  It was Raymond, earl
of Toulouse, who had so far turned Mahometan that he
had no less than three wives in emulation of his Saracen
neighbors beyond the Pyrenees.  An investigation of the
domestic life of Raymond, would have shown it to have been
far more honorable than that of the popes, themselves.  Raymond was therefore arrested on the charge of heresy, of
harboring heretics and placing offices of trust in the hands of
worthy Jews.  His subjects were indignant, for Raymond, it
would seem, was a wise and good ruler and much loved by his
people.

In the disputes that ensued the pope's embassador was
accidentally killed.  Innocent considered this a sufficient reason
for sending into the earl's dominion an army of nearly five
hundred thousand men.  There was no alternative for the earl
but to submit.  He surrendered up his strong places, and even
acknowledged the justice of his punishment.  He was publicly
stripped naked to the waist, and, with a rope around his neck,
led to the altar of the cathedral and there scourged.

But the humiliation and scourging of the earl was not
sufficient to satisfy the soldiery.  They had come for blood and
plunder, and blood and plunder they must have.  Then followed such a scene of horror as tongue or pen cannot describe.
The army was officered by, Roman and French prelates.
Bishops were its generals and an archdeacon its engineer.
The pope's embassador was the commander-in-chief, who,
when asked by a subordinate officer at the battle of Beziers,
how the Catholics might be distinguished from the misbe-

lievers and saved, replied: "Kill them all, God will know
His own in the resurrection."    In the church of St. Mary
Magdalene, seven thousand persons were massacred.   In the

DUNGEON OF THE INQUISITION.

city  twenty thousand more were slaughtered.    The place was
then fired and left as a monument of priestly vengeance.

At the massacre of Levaur four hundred persons were piled together and burned. The embassador, in making up his dispatches to the pope, said that "they made a wonderful blaze, and then went to burn everlastingly in hell."

It was hoped that these horrors would so terrify men that they would never again dare to use the God-given power of reason. The soil had been steeped with the blood of men and the air polluted by their burnings; yet all this did not stifle the truth, nor prevent its growth. Hoping still to effect this, that infernal institution, the Inquisition, was established. Its projectors intended it not only to put an end to public teaching, but also to private thought. When once the Inqustion seized its victim, no person, not even the nearest relative, could converse with him, write to him or intercede for him. He was lost to public view until the hour for his torture or execution had arrived. In Spain alone more than three hundred and forty thousand passed through its terrible ordeal. But this fearful tribunal did not fail to draw upon itself the indignation of men. Such outrages against humanity cannot be perpetrated without bringing retribution in the end.

The great forces which were then at work in society, were well illustrated in the characters of the two leading actors. On one side stands Innocent III., his hands red with the blood of his fellow-men, and hesitating at no atrocity in order to accomplish his purposes.

On the other, was Frederick II., emperor of Germany and Italy. Frederick's early life had been spent in familiar intercourse with Jews and Arabs. In a Saracen university he had received his education; and to his many other accomplishments, he added the speaking of the Arabic as fluently as a Saracen. Jewish and Saracen philosophers had taught him to sneer at the pretensions of the church of Rome: as might be expected he soon came in conflict with her authority.

Between Innocent and Frederick was perpetual enmity; but for a time the conflict was deferred. During this interval the greatness of Frederick was manifested in the internal improvements of his kingdom. He instituted a repressentative assembly or parliament, which by his sanction framed a code of wise and useful laws. This code asserted the principle of equal rights to all, the peasants, the nobles and the church, and an equal proportion of taxation. It also provided for the toleration of all religions, Catholic, Jewish and Mahometan. Frederick emancipated all the serfs and slaves of his dominions, established cheap courts of justice for the poor, and regulated trade and commerce. He even laid down some of those commercial and political maxims recently discussed by Adam Smith and John Stuart Mill, and only in our own times finally received as true. He also established fairs and markets, for the exchange of products, and offered prizes for mechanical improvements and the best breeds of domestic animals. In Naples he founded a great university with liberal provision for worthy but indigent youths. Under him sculpture, painting, poetry and music were liberally patronized, and the Italian tongue first rose to the dignity of a language.

All this was an abomination in the sight of Rome. Gregory IX., succeeded to the pontifical chair in A. D. 1228. Frederick and his parliaments, his laws and universities, his libraries and his toleration were all denounced, and Frederick himself was delivered over to Satan for the good of his soul. For thirty years Frederick combated the power of the church, but he sank in the conflict at last. But the fate of men is by no means an indication of the fate of principles.

> "Truth crushed to earth will rise again,
> The eternal years of God are hers."

Though denounced then, Frederick is now considered one of the benefactors of his race.

Meanwhile an ominous cloud was gathering in the horizon of Rome. The Franciscans, weary of poverty, began to denounce the luxury and corruptions of the regular clergy. At this juncture a strange book make its appearance, which, under the title of "The Everlasting Gospel," struck terror to the hearts of the papal authorities.

It was affirmed that an angel brought it from heaven and gave it to the priest called Cyril, who it was said delivered it to the Abbot Joachim, by whom the book was published. Cyril

had been dead about fifty years when the work first made its
appearance.    According to the admissions of Catholic historians, "The work displayed an enlarged and masterly conception of the historical progress of humanity." It claimed
that 'Romanism had done its work and must now make way
for a new order of ideas.    It proceeded to show that there
are epochs, or ages in the divine government of the world.
During the Jewish dispensation, it had been under the
immediate influence of God the Father.    For the next twelve
hundred years, it had been under the control of God the Son,
but the time has now arrived when the world would be under
the special control of the Holy Spirit.    That man need no
longer treasure up the relics of antiquity, search after the
sayings of the early fathers or even solely and implicitly rely
on the letter of the ancient scriptures, for the Holy Spirit
would manifest itself in visions, dreams and revelations to the
children of men.

One of the grand principles which it taught was, "the
divine right of private judgment."    It asserted that genius
should not be considered an individual possession, but rather
"the gift of God—the visible manifestion of the secret workings of the Holy Spirit for the elevation of the race."    In
short, it taught that "every invention and discovery was only,
in some degree, a revelation of God to man," an unfolding
of the secret laws of nature to man's finite understanding. · It
considered, "those heroes as inspired, who, springing from
society at appointed epochs, displayed a mental or moral power
beyond the ordinary limits of humanity, and around whom, as
around a superior and mysterious power, nations and individuals unhesitatingly gather."

It recognized the hand of God in those grand revolutions,
those great men, those mighty nations, which, arising from
obscurity, communicate a fresh impulse, new vigor and
advanced ideas to the human race.    It was without doubt the
most powerful written work which had appeared since the
days of the apostles.    No wonder the pope, Alexander IV.,
took immediate measures for its destruction.    So far from
being suppressed, its copies were multiplied rapidly, though
printing was as yet unknown.

On the far off plains of Bohemia, among the rugged mountains of the Tyrol, by Alpine torrents and in the valleys of Piedmont, as well as on the distant shores of England and Scotland, its words were carefully read and pondered. In size it was nearly equal to the New Testament, and by many of the humble classes it was reveared as its equal in authority. Many of its truths were conveyed in the form of fable or parable. Historians generally write in the interest of some sect or party, and finding in it little to flatter the pride or vanity of man, have frequently passed it by in silence or have given it merely a passing notice, but it was evidently an instrument in the hands of God for awakening human intellect.

Meanwhile the boundaries of human knowledge were greatly enlarged. Chemistry and medicine had taken their places as established sciences. Roger Bacon, who was born A. D. 1214, had already astonished the learned by his experiments and discoveries in optics, mathematics and chemistry. At the present time it is almost impossible to comprehend the difficulties and perils which then attended every step in experimental science. For example, in making some experiments on the properties of antimony, or stibium, as it was then called, it was found that when given to the swine in their food it increased their fatness with surprising rapidity. But when it was administered to some half-starved monks the poor fellows were every one killed. Hence the modern name of antimony, from *anti*, against, and *moine*, a monk. It may also be added that antimony, whether used as a medicine or in the composition of printer's type for the dissemination of truth is equally unhealthy for sectarian bigots of every description.

Geographical knowledge had also been greatly extended. Adventurous merchants had sailed along both the eastern and western shores of Africa far south of the equator, for they discovered stars and constellations invisible in northern latitudes. The Azores and Canary Islands had been rediscovered after a lapse of more than a thousand years. Portuguese sailors had already made voyages to far off Iceland, the "Ullima Thule" of the ancients. With the exception of north-eastern Asia and southern Africa, the entire boundaries of the eastern continent were known. Marco Polo, in the

3*

interests of Venetian commerce, had explored the vast regions of central Asia, and Moorish merchants of Tripoli, by means of caravans, had trafficked with the tribes of central Africa.

The states of Europe had commenced to assume their modern forms; Portugal had become independent of Spain about A. D. 1139; Switzerland, under Rudolph of Hapsburg, became a distinct nationality in A. D. 1151; Ireland was sub-jugated by Henry II., of England, in A. D. 1172, and British constitutional government commenced by wresting the Magna Charta from King John, in A. D. 1215.

In fine arts we find that Cimabue, who was born in A. D. 1140, and his pupil Giotto, who was born in A. D. 1276, established the Italian school of modern painting.

The foregoing will indicate to some extent the condition of society at the latter end of the thirteenth century. The dark-ness of night had commenced to vanish. The morning star of intelligence had arisen, heralding the coming of a peaceful day—

"A day not cloudless or devoid of storm,
But sunny for the most and clear and warm."

## CHAPTER VIII.

### THE MORNING OF MODERN TIMES.

LESSON FROM HEATHEN MYTHOLOGY — VICISSITUDES OF ROMAN CHURCH—BONIFACE POPE—ADVANCEMENT IN CIVILIZATION—WORK OF THE ROMAN CHURCH—INVEN-TION OF PRINTING—GUTENBERG—BIBLE FIRST PRINTED —COLUMBUS—HIS WONDERFUL DREAM—HIS GREAT VOY-AGE—DISCOVERY OF AMERICA—TRIALS AND TRIUMPHS.

"It breaks—it comes—the misty shadows fly:
A rosy radiance gleams upon the sky;
The mountain tops reflect it calm and clear,
The plain is yet in shade, but day is near."—*Chas. Mackay.*

THE fifteenth century may be justly considered the com-mencement of modern times; for then began the great revolution in science, religion and general knowledge, which has continued until the present time. The time-worn colossus of Rome was tottering under its own weight. Great princes filled the thrones of all the principal countries of Europe. The minds of men seemed awakening as from a sleep. A spirit of scientific research had seized the learned, and a desire for knowledge found its way even to the homes of the lowly.

In every grade of society a new life was in motion. "What an age!" exclaimed Huetton, the religious knight of Germany, "studies flourish, minds are awakening; it is a joy merely to be alive!"

The history of those times cannot be correctly told by a simple recital of facts. This truth should ever be acknowledged, that God is ever present on that vast theatre where successive generations of men meet and struggle. It is true He is unseen; and the unthinking multitude may pass heedlessly by. To the ignorant crowd, the history of the world presents a confused chaos; but to men of thought, it appears as a majestic temple on which the invisible hand of God is at work.

Modern minds might learn a lesson from heathen mythology. The name given by the ancient Greeks to the Deity shows that they had received some primeval revelation of this great truth. He was styled *Zeus*, or the life-giver to all that lives— to nations as well as individuals. From his inspirations Minos and other legislators professed to have received their laws; and on his altars kings and people swore their solemn oaths. This great truth is taught by one of the most beautiful fables of heathen mythology.

Thus *Zeus*, the life-giving principle is the father of *Clio*, the muse of history, whose mother is *Mnemosyne*, or memory. History then is the memory of men's acts and God's providences, and combines a heavenly with an earthly nature. She is the daughter of God and man; but, alas, the purblind philosophy of the ninteenth century has not attained to the lofty views of heathen wisdom!

What a startling fact, that men brought up amid the glorious light of the present age should deny that divine intervention in human affairs which even the very heathens admitted!

The beginning of the fifteenth century finds Boniface IX., on the pontifical throne. During his reign the papal power culminated and began to decline.

No empire of ancient or modern times has experienced such marvelous and varied vicissitudes, as those which have befallen the empire of the Roman church. Born in obscurity and reared in adversity, that church nevertheless succeeded in climbing to a loftier throne and grasping the scepter of a more absolute dominion than either a Xerxes or an Alexander could boast. Pretending to despise mere worldly gains, she cunningly turned the channels of riches towards herself, and emptied them without scruple into her own coffers.

When Boniface ascended the papal throne, the authority of Rome was apparently greater than ever; but in reality it was much undermined by the advancing labors of civilization.

Society had made a great advance in the previous eight hundred years. In the seventh century, a cloud of more than Egyptian darkness overshadowed Europe. Then it was occupied by wandering savages; now it was organized into families, neighborhoods and cities. The seventh century left it full of bondmen; the fifteenth found it without a slave. Where there had been trackless forests there were now the abodes of civilized men. Instead of bloody chieftains drinking out of their enemies' skulls, there were grave professors teaching the laws of nature and the principles of science.

Nor was this all. Rome herself had a preparatory work to do, and had she confined herself to that work, and sought not to trammel the minds of men, she would have continued a blessing to the race. Never before in the history of the world was there such a system. From her central seat she could equally take in a hemisphere at a glance or examine the private life of any individual. In all Europe there was not a man too great or too obscure, too insignificant or too desolate for her. Surrounded by her solemnities every one received his name at her altar; her bells chimed at his marriage; and her knell tolled at his funeral. When even to his friends his lifeless corpse had become an offense, she received it into her consecrated ground, there to rest until the great reckoning day. In times of lawlessness and rapine, she sheltered the helpless from the tyrant, and made her sanctuaries a refuge for the despairing and oppressed. But like all man-made systems of religion, she failed by attempting to enforce fixed laws on society in the presence of higher truths and advancing civilization.

During all these centuries mankind had slowly but surely advanced and Abraham's seed, the Jews and Saracens, had been the leaders of that progress. Quietly the materials had been gathering until the whole continent was ripe for revolution.

Meanwhile God had raised up instruments, by which the commerce, politics and religious thought of Europe were completely changed.

In A. D. 1484, there were living in various parts of Europe three persons who were destined to set in motion these mighty movements. These were Gutenberg, Columbus and Luther. Around these men cluster many notable events; and a history of their lives and times would include some of the brightest pages in the annals of our race.

Gutenberg was then an old man living at Mentz, in Germany. His broad shoulders, well knit frame and strong arms showed that he was acquainted with labor, and capable of great endurance. His broad and full forehead indicated a man of reflective mind and inventive faculty. His keen, full grey eye revealed a soul full of earnestness, intelligence and power. He had conferred on mankind the most useful invention, since Cadmus, nearly three thousand years ago, taught the barbarian Greeks the art of writing. This invention was the art of printing, which has been such a mighty instrument for the transmission of thought, and the civilization of the world. The Saracens had already invented the art of making paper from linen rags. Previous to this, parchment was the only substance well adapted for writing upon. Paper-making and printing produced great changes in the manufacture of books. By the one, books were greatly cheapened, by the other, greatly multiplied. Thought could now be transmitted cheaply and swiftly in a thousand different directions. Priestcraft saw the danger, and, terrified lest truth should emerge, immediately attempted to control and restrain the press.    At this time the art of printing was known to only five or six persons.    It is curious to observe that even war was the means of quickening the growth and extension of this wonderful art.    In 1462, the storming of Mentz dispersed Gutenberg and his co-workers and gave the secret to the world.    In A. D. 1465, it appeared in Italy; in 1469, in France; in 1474, Caxton brought it to England, and in 1477 it was introduced in Spain.

Meanwhile Pope Alexander VI., excommunicated all printers not licensed by him, and an order was issued to burn all books not recommended by the papal authorities.    But these frantic struggles of the powers of darkness were unavailing.    Lovers of books were gratified by seeing them multiplied by thousands. The Bibe was printed as early as 1454, and was followed shortly afterwards by other important books.

The power of the press continued to increase, until at the present time it is without doubt the most powerful aid to modern civilization.

At the beginning of the fifteenth century a profound ignorance prevailed concerning the western regions of the Atlantic. Its vast waters were regarded with awe and wonder; and though from time to time, pieces of carved wood and other relics of Indian skill had floated to the shores of the old world, giving to its wondering inhabitants evidences of land beyond the watery horizon, yet no one ventured to spread a sail and seek that land veiled in mystery and peril.

Columbus was the first who had the inspiration to conceive and the heroic courage to brave the mysteries of this perilous deep.    He unfolded to the wandering gaze of the inhabitants of Europe a new hemisphere, and opened it to their spirit of discovery and enterprise—opened it also, alas, to their cupidity and cruelty!

Christopher Columbus was born in the city Genoa, about 1447, and became one of the most remarkable men of any land or time.    Having carefully studied the sciences of geography and astronomy he became convinced that the earth was not flat, as most men then believed, but was really a vast globe or ball.    He perceived that when the moon was eclipsed, the shadow which the earth cast upon the moon was round; and he reasoned that as the shadow was round, the object that made that shadow must be round also.

He visited the great Saracen schools in Spain, and there received additional proof of this truth. Spain, was then a great maritime nation, and there he conversed with great sea-captains whose voyages were already attracting the attention of the learned. He himself also made a voyage to far off Iceland, and possibly to Greenland, to which country the pope had already sent a bishop and several missionaries.

CHRISTOPHER COLUMBUS.

In A. D. 1485, when Columbus was about thirty-eight years of age he made his first application to the king of Portugal for aid in his great scheme of maritime discovery, but without success. He then successively applied to Spain, Genoa, Venice and England.

But the monarchs of Europe were under the control of Rome, and therefore too busy in aiding her religious persecutions to listen to the appeals of science.

Indeed in the very year in which Columbus made his first application, the Inquisition put to death nearly seventeen thousand persons, besides imprisoning thirty-two thousand more. Nor was this all, ninety-two thousand Jews had suffered confiscation of their property, and had been given the unenviable choice of death, banishment or perpetual slavery. And the Saracens, who had dwelt in Spain for more than seven hundred years, or nearly twice as long a time as has elapsed since the discovery of America, were expelled from the lands which they had so long cultivated and beautified, and from their cities which had so long led the world in the arts, sciences and general civilization.

One evening in the autumn of A. D. 1485, a man of majestic appearance, pale, care-worn, and though in the meridian of life, with silver hair, leading a little boy by the hand, asked alms at the gate of a Franciscan convent near Polos—not for himself, but only a little bread and water for his child. That man was Columbus, destined to startle the inhabitants of Europe with the discovery of a new continent. But he was obliged to wait until he could take advantage of the commercial rivalry of Spain and Portugal.

The trade of Eastern Asia had always been a source of immense wealth to the nations that had controlled it. For more than a thousand years Venice had held the keys to that commerce. As discoveries extended, other nations perceived the possibility of opening new routes to the East and thus rivaling the commercial greatness of Venice. One of these plans was to sail around the southern end of Africa, the other to sail directly westward across the Atlantic. It was plain to every thinking person that if India could be reached by sailing westward, maritime power would pass from the Mediterranean countries to those upon the Atlantic coast.

About this time Columbus had a wonderful dream, or vision. An unknown voice spoke to him, and said: "God will cause thy name to be wonderfully resounded throughout the earth; and will give thee the keys to the ocean which are held with strong chains." From this time forward, Columbus looked upon himself as chosen from among men to accomplish the purposes of heaven; to bring the ends of the earth together, that all nations, and peoples, and tongues might be united under the banner of the Redeemer.

Isabella and Ferdinand were then joint king and queen of Spain. Meanwhile, Columbus had gained many influential friends, among whom was a Jewish sea-faring family named Pinzon, and Luis de Santangel the spiritual adviser of Queen Isabella.

At this time Columbus seemed more likely to fall into the hands of the Inquisition and suffer for his heresy than to succeed in his great enterprise.

At this juncture Luis de Santangel obtained audience with the queen, and addressed her with all the energy of a man who speaks for the last time in behalf of a favored project. Isabella listened attentively, hesitated a moment and then pledged her jewels to raise the amount necessary for the expedition. Contemporary writers have been enthusiastic in their descriptions of Isabella; but time has sanctioned their eulogies. She is one of the purest and most beautiful characters on the pages of history.

At length, on the 17th of April, A. D. 1492, Columbus was ushered into the royal presence, and received his commission. Immediately he commenced preparations, and on the 3rd of August, 1492, set sail on his ever-memorable voyage. The expedition consisted of three small vessels: the *Santa Maria*, commanded by Columbus; the *Pinta*, by Martin Alonzo Pinzon; and the *Nina*, by Vincent Yanez Pinzon. "The Pinzons were doubly interested in this voyage, for while they sought for a new and profitable route of commerce, they doubtless also felt a desire to find an asylum for their persecuted Jewish brethren." (See Lovel's American History, Canadian edition.)

Having touched at the Canary Islands they sailed directly westward. On losing sight of the last trace of land the hearts of the crews failed them. Behind them was everything dear to the heart of man: country, family, friends, life itself; before them everything was chaos, mystery and peril.

Columbus tried in every way to soothe their distress and inspire them with his own glorious anticipations. He described to them the magnificent countries to which he was about to conduct them: the islands of the Indian seas, teeming with gold and precious stones; the regions of Mangi and Cathay with their cities of unrivalled wealth and splendor. Nor were these promises made for purposes of deception. Columbus evidently believed that he would realize them all.

For many days they were gently but speedily waffed over a tranquil sea, but when near the middle of the Atlantic, they, for the first time, observed the variation of the needle of the compass, which no longer pointed directly north, but had veered around and pointed in a somewhat different direction.

SHIPS OF COLUMBUS.

Columbus was greatly perplexed yet dared not communicate his thoughts to anyone. It seemed as if the very laws of nature were changing, as they advanced, and they were entering another world subject to unknown influences; that the compass was about to lose its mysterious virtue, and without that guide what was to become of them on a vast and trackless ocean? Columbus gave an explanation of this phenomenon which satisfied the crew though unsatisfactory to himself. His situation was daily becoming more critical in proportion as they approached the regions where he expected to find land. At length, on the 9th of October, the crew broke out in open mutiny and threatened to throw him overboard, designing then

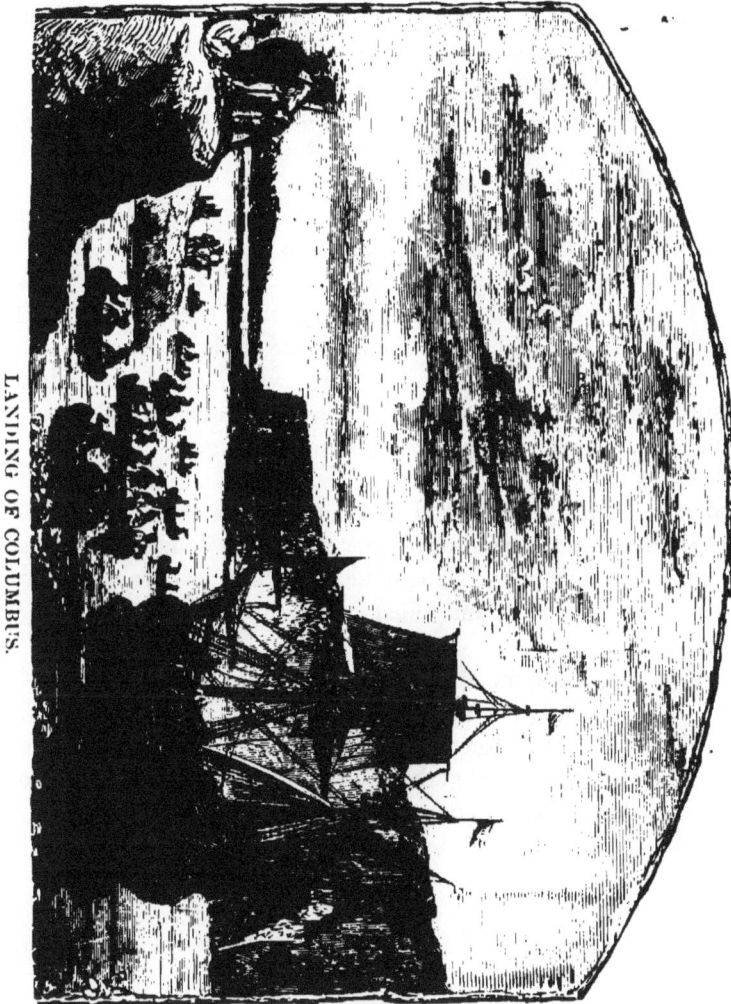

LANDING OF COLUMBUS.

to return to Spain. A compromise was effected, that if they would continue to sail westward three days longer, and no land was discovered he would then return. Two days passed away and still no sight of land.

On the evening of the second day, Columbus remained on deck. What were the feelings that pervaded his breast no one but God can tell; with nothing but the heaving ocean beneath him and the silent stars o'er head. Anxiously he stands upon the prow of his vessel and peers into the darkness. It is one o'clock! Suddenly a gleam as of a torch is seen in the horizon! Is it a flash of phosphoric light as is sometimes seen on the surface of these tropical seas, or is it a blaze of fire indicating the habitations of men?

Soon the joyful cry of "Ho! land, ho!" resounded throughout the ship, and the booming of cannon announced the discovery to the other vessels.

When the dawning of the morning came, they beheld in all their grandeur and beauty, the hills and valleys, streams and forests of a new world. The men who had been so lately mutinous now came forward and bowed down before Columbus, and did homage to him as though he were a god.

Trials before triumphs have ever been the lot of self-taught men, and will be to the end of time. If the chosen heroes of this earth were counted over, they would be found to be men who stood alone and labored and waited; while those for whom they agonized and toiled poured upon them contumely and scorn.

The very martyrs of the past who were hooted at, reviled and spit upon by the mob, are the ones who are honored now. They suffered cruel tortures and burnings; to-day, the children of this generation are gathering up their scattered ashes to deposit them in the golden urn of a nation's history.

# CHAPTER IX.

## INFLUENCE OF ISRAEL—DISCOVERERS AND REFORMERS.

HISTORY IN WORDS—BRITISH COAT OF ARMS—THE TEN TRIBES—ACCOUNT OF ESDRAS—DISPERSION OF THE TRIBES—MIXED SEED OF ISRAEL—EFFECT ON EUROPEAN SOCIETY—JEWISH INFLUENCE—DISCOVERY OF CAPE OF GOOD HOPE—PACIFIC OCEAN DISCOVERED—MAGELLAN'S VOYAGE—DISCOVERS CAPE HORN—DISTANCE SAILED— DEATH OF MAGELLEN—VOYAGE COMPLETED—ITS EFFECT ON THE PUBLIC—HUSS AND JEROME BURNED—JOHN ZISKA—PERSECUTIONS OF WALDENSES—CAPTURE OF MENTZ—DISPERSION OF PRINTERS—HANS BOHEIM—JOSS FRITZ—SALE OF INDULGENCES—MARTIN LUTHERBURNS THE POPE'S LETTER—GRAND COUNCIL AT WORMS— ROME IN A RAGE—LUTHER KIDNAPPED.

ONE of the most pleasing and at the same time instructive amusements in which a thoughtful mind can engage, is to trace the derivation of certain words of our language to the primitive times and people where they originated, and thus learn the social and mental condition of the people who first used them.     It is pleasing to know that *dish* and *mop, mat* and *rug,* and other household terms are the very words that were spoken by the women of ancient Britian, two thousand years ago, and have been handed down from generation to generation, with little or no variation.     In like manner the words *ax, plow, house, post, bed, fire,* and hundreds of others, can be easily discerned under the old Saxon forms.     And as these words are precisely those that would be used by a rude or half-civilized people, while those words that refer to a more advanced state of society cannot be traced to our Saxon ancestors we may correctly infer the extent of their knowledge and social condition.    Further, as the ancient British words refer to domestic affairs while those of Saxon origin refer exclusively to the avocations of man, we can easily perceive that the Anglo-Saxon tongue has originated from the marriage of the ancient British women with their Saxon conquerors.

Hence Max Muller, the learned professor of languages, in the university at Oxford, England, very justly remarks that "by means of philology we have a more accurate record of our race than any narrative written by prejudice or ill-informed historians."

Now it is generally admitted that Germans, Anglo-Saxons and men descended from these nationalities, in one word, German thought, led the van of progress in science, literature and religious thought, during the fourteenth, fifteenth and sixteenth centuries, and in fact has continued to do so up to the present time.

From the fifth century, when Attila, king of the Huns, declared himself "The scourge of God," wave after wave of conquest by these hardy warriors had swept over the hills and plains of western and southern Europe, until their blood and their love of civil and religious liberty were infused into every European nation.

Now the language of the Goths, or ancient Germans, plainly indicates that they were not the primitive people of Europe, but had conquered and intermingled with them in the same manner as the Saxons conquered and intermingled with the inhabitants of ancient Britain, or the Spaniards with those of Mexico.

But it may be asked, whence came they?    In this connection two other questions may also be asked:  why is it that the German language contains so many idioms and terms that bear a close relationship to the language of the ancient Hebrews and Chaldeans?    (*See Max Muller's lectures on language.*)    And why is it that the lion, which was the emblem of Judah, and the unicorn, which was the emblem of Israel, are in modern times, emblazoned on the coat of arms of England?    (*See Ant. of Jews by Josephus, also Num. xxiii.,* 22 *and Deut. xxxiii,* 17.)    These questions are worthy of deep and careful consideration; and to better understand them it will be necessary to briefly trace the history of the children of Israel.

As is well known, after the death of Solomon the kingdom was divided into two parts, known as the kingdom of Judah and the kingdom of Israel. In 730 B. C., Hashem, king of Israel, became tributary to Shalmaneser, king of Assyria. Nine years later his capital was taken and the greater portion of the people were carried away captive beyond the river Euphrates, and people from other countries were put in possession of their inheritance. In the Apocrapha the Prophet Esdras states that these ten tribes went a journey of a year and a half into the north country. He says: "These are the ten tribes which were carried away prisoners out of their own land in the time of Hosea the king, whom Shalmaneser the king of Assyria led away captive; and he carried them over the waters so they came into another land. But they took this council among themselves, that they would leave the multitude of the heathen and go forth into a farther country where never mankind dwelt, that they might there keep their statutes which they never kept in their own land. For through that country there was a great way to go, namely, in a year and a half's journey, and the same region is called Arsareth." (*II. Esdras, xiii*, 40, 41, 42 and 45.)

Now by looking on a map of the eastern continent it will be seen at once that the Black Sea and the Caucasus mountains lie directly north of the river Euphrates. It is quite possible that the Black Sea is the "waters" to which Esdras refers. Also Josephus, in speaking of the return of the Jews under Esdras, says, "Many of them took their effects with them and came to Babylon, as very desirous of going down to Jerusalem, but then the entire body of the people of Israel remained in that country, wherefore there are but two tribes in Asia and Europe subject to the Romans, while the ten tribes are beyond the Euphrates till now, and are an immense multitude and not to be estimated by numbers." (*Ant. Book II. chapter 5.*)

Perhaps the words of the ancient Roman are not altogether fable when he says that "Beyond the Borean (Caucasus) Mountains live a people who are sublime in their virtue since they dwell very distant form the provinces, in great simplicity and give great heed to the oracles which their gods have given unto them." Thus we have not only the sure word of prophecy, but likewise the admission of heathen writers.

Max Muller, in his work on language, in referring to the migrations of ancient European tribes, says, "Two great routes lay before them, one by way of the valleys of the Don and Volga across modern Russia to the shores of the Baltic, the other along the shores of the Black Sea to the valley of the Danube."

He also demonstrates the close relationship that exists between the Hebrew language and the language of the people of Finland in western Russia. Considering that more than twenty-five centuries have rolled by since the dispersion of Israel, sufficient time has elapsed for mighty changes. Muller adds in another place, "The time was when the ancestors of the Indians, the Fins, the Slavonic and German tribes of central Europe and the modern English lived in one enclosure, nay, under the same roof."

In the latter part of the second century or beginning of the third, these new settlers had spread as far westward as the Danube, and settled in the Roman province of Dacia, which lay on the north bank of that river. They also asked permission to cross the river which was granted under certain stipulations.

Still they continued to increase in numbers, and by intermarriage with the native tribes had in the fifth century become formidable enemies of Rome and under the name of Dacians, Huns, Vandals, Ostrogoths, Visigoths, Suevi and Heruli precipitated themselves upon Italy and wreaked a terrible vengeance.

The history of some of these, as the Huns for example, may be traced to the second century before the Christian era and to the very locality indicated by the Prophet Esdras and by Josephus. For over twenty-six centuries these scattered tribes have continued to mix up with the nations of the earth, but in their long migrations westward they have lost many of their distinctive characteristics.

Doubtless it is from this mixed seed of Israel that many, aye nearly all, the great reformers, inventors and discoverers have sprung. This infusion of new blood had a marked effect on the nations of western Europe, but more especially on Italy, which had continued to decline, from the days of Augustus, until these nations mingled with the degenerate ancient race, and infused new life into her decaying civilization. The result was that a succession of poets, painters, sculptors, philosophers, inventors and discoverers sprung up in Italy and western Europe unparalleled in the history of the world. Above all, the invention of printing had just come in time to spread whatever new ideas were afloat, with a rapidity never known before. In fifty-two years from the time of that invention came the discovery of America. Five years later two Jewish priests, Rabbi Abraham, and Rabbi Joseph, brought to King John II., of Portugal, a Saracen map of the entire coast of Africa.

Thus instructed King John sent out several expeditions in one of which Brazil was accidentally discovered. Aided by this, Vasco de Gama set sail, and on Nov. 20th, 1497, rounded the cape of Good Hope. Sixteen years later Balboa discovered the Pacific Ocean, and six years still later, or in A. D. 1519, Magellan set out on his memorable voyage to circumnavigate the world.

The story of that voyage of wild adventure seems never to grow old by repeating. The narrative of that voyage is too long for this brief sketch, but a few items may not be out of place.

After many months of sailing in strange seas, he at length discovered a new land to which he gave the name of Patagonia. Here he found giants clad in skins, one of whom was greatly terrified at seeing his own image in a looking-glass.

His perseverance was at last rewarded, and after fifteen months of struggling and adventures he discovered Cape Horn, passed through the strait which now bears his name and entered the Great South Sea, on Nov. 28th, 1520. An eye-witness relates that he shed tears of joy when he recognized its great expanse, and that God had brought him where he might grapple with its unknown dangers. Admiring its placid

THE STRAITS OF MAGELLAN.

surface he courteously gave it the name it will ever bear, the "Pacific Ocean." Magellan was the first European to discover that when the nights are long in the northern hemisphere they are correspondingly short in the southern. When he passed through the straits the nights were only four hours long. At the same time in Spain they were nearly fifteen hours long. And now the great sailor having burst through the barrier of the great American continent steered for the north-west. For three months and fifteen days he sailed on and on, but saw no inhabited land.

He and his crew were compelled by famine to soak old leather in the sea, then boil it and make of it a wretched food; and to drink water that had become putrid by keeping; yet he resolutely held his course, though his men were dying daily. He estimated that he sailed over this unknown sea more than twelve thousand miles.

In the whole history of human undertakings there is nothing that exceeds, if indeed there is anything that equals, this voyage of Magellan. That of Columbus dwindles away in comparison. It is a display of super-human courage and perseverance, an exhibition of heroic resolution, not to be diverted from its purpose by any motive, or any suffering, but inflexibly persisting to its end.

This unparalleled resolution met its reward at last. He reached the Ladrones, a group of islands north of the equator. Thence he sailed to the Spice Islands, where he met with European merchants. He had accomplished his object and proven that the earth was round. At an island called Zebu, or Mutan, he was murdered either by the natives or by his own men. In a few days more his crew learned that they were actually in the vicinity of their friends. On the morning of Nov. 8th, 1521, they entered Tidore, the capital of the Spice Islands, and the king swore upon the Koran alliance to the sovereign of Spain.

Magellan's crew continued their voyage amid hardships and perils, and at length, on Sept. 10th, 1522, the good ship, *San Vittoria*, sailed into the very port from which she had departed just three years and twenty-seven days before. She had accomplished the greatest achievement in the history of the human race. She had circumnavigated the earth. Magellan lost his life in his great enterprise, but he made his name immortal. His lieutenant Sebastian d'Elcano received the proudest and noblest medal ever given to a sailor. It was a golden globe belted with this inscription, *Primus circumdedisti me*—"Thou hast first circumnavigated me."

At the present time it is almost impossible to conceive the effect of Magellan's voyage had upon the public mind. One of the leading dogmas of Rome had been that the earth was flat. Now it was proved that the earth was indeed a vast ball. If Rome had been in error in this case, where was her infallibility? Might not some of her other teachings be equally false? Many leading minds began to doubt her authority. Even Pope Leo X., is said to have become skeptical. At all events he chose to spend his leisure time in his library reading to his sister out of the beautiful new printed books which were then throwing a flood of intellectual light on all grades of society. The philosophy of Aristotle and Plato, the poems of Homer and Virgil, the sciences of the Saracens and the narratives of the adventures of Columbus and Vasco de Gama had more charms for him than burning and torturing heretics as his predecessors had done.

While science was undermining the influence of Rome in one direction, religious thought was busy at work in another. That great religious revolution commonly called the Reformation had long been gathering its forces; and already sounded from behind the Alps the loud clarion of battle.

The memory of John Huss and Jerome of Prague was still fresh in the minds of the populace. Huss had been burned at Constance, in A. D. 1415, and Jerome the year following. When the news of these barbarous executions reached Bohemia, it threw the whole kingdom into confusion and a civil war was kindled from the ashes of the martyrs.

John Ziska, the leader of the populace, collected an army of forty thousand men and defeated the emperor, Sigismund, in several battles. When Ziska found that he was dying, he gave orders that his skin should be made into a drum which was long the symbol of victory to his followers.

The Waldenses also who dwelt in the valleys of Switzerland and Piedmont had lively memories of cruel wrongs. Their

THE RACK.

ancestors had been destroyed by Pope Innocent III., and as late as A. D. 1487, they had been driven to the mountains and obliged to wander there until their feeble and little ones were left buried in the Alpine snows.    No wonder they chanted that grand old hymn, commencing:

"O God, arise, avenge Thy slaughtered Saints,
Whose bones lie bleaching on the Alpine mountains cold."

The writings of Dante and Petrarch, Reuchlin and Erasmus, were already scattered in every direction, by means of the printing press, and wielded a mighty influence in society.

The siege and capture of Mentz, in A. D. 1462, had the effect of scattering Guttenberg and his co-workers.  Printing presses were established immediately afterwards in Italy, Spain, Portugal, Holland, France and England.

In 1476, on the banks of the river Maine, in central Germany had appeared a strange character named Hans Boheim. He professed to be a prophet of God, to have received visions, and to have been sent to proclaim that the kingdom of heaven was at hand.   More than forty thousand men flocked to his standard.   At length the bishops of Mentz and Wurtzburg interfered, dispersed the crowd and burned the prophet.   He was but a sign of the times—"a voice crying in the wilderness."   His memory was not forgotten.   In 1493, another movement took place, and again in 1501.   Maximilian, the emperor of Germany, ordered the leaders to be quartered alive and their wives and children to be banished.   But the fire was only slumbering.   In 1512, it commenced again on a larger scale.   It found a leader in Joss Fritz, a soldier of commanding presence and great natural eloquence, used to battle and above all to patience.   He was one of those who had escaped being quartered.   His banner was blue silk with a white cross, and underneath the motto, "O Lord, help the righteous."   Fritz was the William Tell of his times.   No wonder his name is a favorite one among the Germans.

These conflicts, commonly known as the "Wars of the Peasants," had shown the masses that with more union and better information they were the real strength of the nation.

Such was the condition of affairs in the very locality where, four years afterwards, burst forth the great religious revolution known as the Reformation.

Society seemed waiting for a coming man of strong will and fervent religious nature, who should give something of organization to those movements, and gather around him an irresistable phalanx of the noble, the learned and ardent spirits of the age. This man was Martin Luther. He came from his cell a shaven monk, in his hand no sceptre, on his head no crown. But he had a human heart within him ; and it gushed out for human woe.

Strong in the principles of right he hurled the firebrands of truth right and left and kindled such a flame that all the waves of error could never quench it.

The immediate cause of the Reformation was when John Tetzel, in 1574, was sent into Germany to sell indulgences.

The church of Rome had long taught the people that the pope and clergy under him held the keys of heaven. At this time the pope was in need of means to complete that great cathedral called St. Peter's Church. He therefore issued indulgences or pardons for all kinds of sins. These pardons or indulgences entitled whoever bought them to a free passport to heaven. Nor was this all. A man of sufficient wealth could purchase the pardon of a sin he *intended* to commit. Thus the civil law was shorn of its power and the nation of its wealth.

This bold blasphemy provoked the indignation of a people already ripe for revolution.

Luther, then thirty-four years of age, began to denounce the sale of these indulgences. In 1520, the pope issued a decree, or bull, as it was called, condemning Luther and his writings. Luther in turn defied the pope. When the news reached him he took the decree and all the Roman books he could find, and on December 10, 1520, burned them in a public place just outside the walls of the city of Wittenberg. Then Luther was summoned to appear before a grand council, or court, to be held in the city of Worms. His friends procured him a passport or pledge of security, lest the papal authorities should take his life.

Accordingly, on the 17th of April, 1521, Luther appeared before the council, or diet, as it was called. The Emperor Charles V., of Germany, presided in person. When Luther was asked to recant his opinions and deny his own teachings, he not only refused to do so but also pleaded his own cause

with eloquence and power.   So powerful were his arguments
that many of the nobility were won over to his side.   A poor
monk, the son of a simple peasant, clad in the armor of truth,
had defied and defeated the proudest potentates of earth!   No
wonder that Rome was in a rage!   No wonder that the friends
of Luther deemed it advisable to kidnap him and carry him
away to the castle of Wartburg, in the solitudes of the Thur-
ingian forest!   No wonder that those valiant knights, Ulrich
von Hutten and Franz von Sickingen, prepared to use their
swords and eloquence in defense of right!   We may not in all
things admire the character of Luther or defend his acts; yet
no grander figure appears on the pages of modern history than
Luther, as, with one hand upon his breast and the other lifted
towards heaven, he refused the emperor's demand to retract
his writings or deny the truth, closing with these memorable
words, "*Hier stehe ich, Gott helfe mir.  Amen.*"   "Here I
stand, God help me.   Amen."

The battle that Luther fought was not only for Germany
and the sixteenth century, but for all countries, all peoples and
all coming times.   It was a battle not merely against the
pope, but against all powers religious or secular, that seek to
enchain the human mind or prevent the free exercise of
religion.

# CHAPTER X.

## RESULTS OF THE REFORMATION.

GERMANY AROUSED—PEASANTS' WAR—MUNTZER'S PROCLAMA-
TION—EMPEROR QUARRELS WITH THE POPE—RESULTS
IN OTHER COUNTRIES—GROWTH OF MODERN LANGUAGES
—LUTHER'S CROWNING WORK—POWER OF SUPERSTITION--
WITCHCRAFT—REFORMERS NOT INSPIRED—EXTRACTS
FROM MOSHEIM—BATTLE-AX OF GOD—COPERNICUS—
GALILEO—NEWTON—DEATH OF BRUNO—CHANGE IN
COMMERCIAL AFFAIRS—SPANISH ARMADA—BLESSED BY
THE POPE—DESTROYED BY A STORM—ITS EFFECT ON
EUROPE--ENGLAND'S INFLUENCE AND POSITION—
AMERICA THE LAND OF REFUGE.

AS the booming of cannon, announcing the begining of
battle echoes and re-echoes far and wide, so did the result
of the council, or diet, in the city of Worms. The answer of
Luther was repeated by thousands of sympathizing friends.
Instead of growing fainter as it died away in the distance, it
increased in intensity and power, till its echoes reverberated
through every valley, and over every hill-top in central
Germany.

Within twenty-four hours Ulrich von Hutten and Franz von
Sickingen had mustered four hundred armed knights and eight
thousand foot soldiers all ready to fight, or, if need be, to die
for the principles Luther had advocated. The commotion continued until it culminated in a civil war, in A. D. 1525. The
horrors of that war no tongue can tell. Nightly the papal
party burned at the stake the prisoners they had taken. Amid
the groans of wounded and dying peasants on the battle field
around them, and the drunken revelry of the camp, might be
heard the laughter of the nobles as they watched the struggles
and heard the shrieks of their victims as they slowly roasted
to death. But the révolution continued to spread. The rage of

4*

the peasants, who had so long been crushed by the iron heel of oppression, knew no bounds. A few extracts from the proclamation of their leader, Munzer, may not be out of place, as they indicate to some extent the nature of the conflict then going on!

"Arise and fight the battle of the Lord! On! on! on! Now is the time; the wicked tremble when they hear of you. Be pitiless! Heed not the groans of the impious! Rouse up ye townsmen and villagers; above all, rouse up ye free men of the mountains! On! on! on! while the fire is burning, while the warm sword is yet reeking with the slaughter! Give the fire no time to go out, the sword no time to cool! Kill all the proud ones! While they reign over you it is no time to talk of God! Amen.

"Given at Muhlhausen, 1525.

"THOMAS MUNZER,

"servant of God against the wicked."

Such was the character of the men with whom the pope had to deal. At length the emperor, Charles V., found it politic to side with his people. Meanwhile Clement VII., succeeded to the papal throne, in 1523. The emperor and the new pope soon quarrelled, and, in 1527, a German army acting under the direction of the German emperor captured and sacked the imperial city of Rome, and more pitilessly pillaged it than it had been a thousand years before by the Goths and Vandals. From this time Rome ceased to be the capital of the professedly Christian world.

But the revolution stayed not here. Its principles of reform passed over the Alps and found a hearty welcome among the hardy mountaineers of Switzerland. It reached the Rhine and with the current of that mighty river flowed onward to the sea. The sturdy sons of Holland received its teachings; and the patient peasantry of Denmark, Norway and Sweden accepted it as an improvement on the past.

Germany continued in the throes of revolution for more than thirty years, or until the peace of Augsburg, in 1555.

In the meantime England had revolted from Rome, in 1532; Denmark followed in 1538; Geneva in 1541; Norway and Sweden in 1550; Scotland in 1560; and Holland in 1581.

Never in the history of the world was fulfilled more literally the words that our Savior said in reference to the truth: "Think not that I am come to send peace on earth: I came not to send peace but a sword," etc. (*See Matt. x.* 34, 38.) For more than a hundred years Europe continued to be the theatre of civil wars, until the nations were completely exhausted—in some cases their power and influence permanently weakened.

We might in view of its immedite results, be inclined to look upon the Reformation as producing more evil than good. Yet amid the wars, bloodshed, anarchy and persecutions, society made rapid steps in the path of progress.

The Reformation promoted national growth, and mental activity. During the middle ages, the various nations of Europe were in the condition of colonies to a vast religious empire whose center and seat of government was Rome. But after the peace at Augsburg, 1555, all this was changed. Each nation that accepted the Reformation, became socially and religiously as well as politically free. Rome was shorn of her power. She was no longer the supreme court of appeal; nor did the high dignitaries of those realms look to her for preferment.

The Reformation was obviously only partially successsful. Where it succeeded it infused new energy; where it failed it produced reaction. Those nations that rejected the light, glimmering though it was, fell back into the double bondage of kingcraft and priestcraft. The Bastile of France was a symbol of the one; the Inquisition of Spain a type of the other. Wave after wave of revolution has swept over these unhappy countries. The guilty streets of Paris and Madrid have been deluged with blood until their population has sunk down into religious apathy or brazen infidelity.

In no particular was the effect of the Reformation more apparent than in the impulse it gave to national languages and literature. Latin had been the language of the Roman empire and Roman church. But when the nations revolted from this central authority they immediately began to cultivate their own native tongues. Learning was no longer confined to the few, nor communicated through the medium of a foreign language, but became the heritage of the people.

The crowning work of Luther was in giving to the German people his German Bible and hymns. The earnest, vigorous German in which they were written fixed the future style of the language. The classic German of to-day is the German of Luther's Bible, and Luther's hymns.

In England, too, the same thing is to be marked. The English translation of the Bible, together with other works of that era, such as Shakspeare's dramas, Milton's poems and Bunyan's Pilgrim's Progress, have done more to stamp the character of our modern English than all later publications.

It may be asked, Why did not the human mind, in this era, free itself from its trammels, claim its true freedom and concede it to every one? The answer is, the range of knowledge was too narrow. The minds of men could not take a broader view of things than the horizon of their knowledge let them. Ignorance and superstition still held a terrible sway.

It is true that the whole character of that age bears the stamp of the German rather than the Italian intellect. It was the energy of a Luther, the learning and loving heart of a Melanchthon, the polished wit of an Erasmus, which then gave impulse and direction to the thoughts and opinions of the world, much more than the frivolous jesting of the infidel priests who thronged the streets of Rome and the halls of the Vatican. Yet even these great men were controlled by superstition, to a very great extent. Witchcraft was universally believed in at that time. Hundreds, aye thousands, of unoffending old women, with no other fault than that they were poor and old, were burned to death as witches, instead of being treated with that respect due to those who have lived many years and spent their best days for the good of others.

Social eminence was no safeguard against these delusions. When it was affirmed that Agnes Sampson, with two hundred other witches, had sailed in sieves from Leith to North Berwick church to hold a banquet with the devil, James I., had the torture applied to the wretched woman, and took pleasure in putting appropriate questions to her. It then was charged that the two hundred old women had baptized and then drowned a black cat, thereby raising a dreadful storm in which the ship that carried the king narrowly escaped being wrecked. Upon this, Agnes was condemned to the flames. She died protesting her innocence, and piteously calling on Jesus to have mercy on her for Christian men would not.

Of all the early reformers, Luther and Melanchthon were perhaps the freest from superstition, and yet even they devoutly believed that in the Tiber, not far distant from the pope's palace, a monster had been found having the head of an ass, the body of a man and the claws of a bird. After searching their Bibles to find out what the prodigy meant, they at length concluded that it was one of the signs and wonders which were to precede the fall of the papacy, and published a pamphlet about it. Yet Luther and Melanchthon were the leaders of a great movement, the teachers of a great nation, and were in every respect the most influential persons in that nation. The people, credulous and grossly ignorant, listened and believed. We, at this distance of time and living in another realm of thought, can form but a faint conception of the effect these horrible conceits produced upon them.

But the greatest need of those times was the want of divine authority. The writings of Luther, Melanchthon, Erasmus and Calvin were never considered as inspired. Luther himself never professed to have divine authority for his teachings; but on the other hand denounced the very idea of inspiration.

When, in 1525, Munzer and his associates (commonly known as the prophets of Zwickaw) claimed divine authority, Luther was foremost in denouncing and persecuting them, and their followers. According to Mosheim, their principal crimes were in denying infant baptism and the right of a distinct class to preach for hire; and asserting that "God still continued to reveal His will to chosen persons by dreams and visions." (See Mosheim Vol. II., p. 128.) They also claimed "that God in His own good time would erect to Himself a holy church possessing a perfect organization, and would set apart for the execution of this grand design, a certain number of chosen instruments divinely assisted and prepared for this chosen work, by the aid and inspiration of His Holy Spirit." As a consequence they claimed the right to rebaptizing persons coming from other churches.

Mosheim further admits, "The extreme difficulty of correcting or influencing by the prospect of suffering, or even by the terrors of death, minds that are firmly bound by the ties of religion. In almost all the countries of Europe, an unspeakable number of those unhappy people preferred death, in its worst forms, to a retraction of their opinions. Neither the view of the flames that were kindled to consume them, nor the ignominy of the gibbet, nor the terrors of the sword, could shake their invincible constancy or make them abandon tenets that appeared dearer to them than life itself and all its enjoyments." (*See Mosheim Vol. II., p.* 131.)

To this sect and its principles Luther was bitterly opposed, but this opposition argues nothing in his favor, nor does it strengthen his authority. It may also be added that if Rome had divine authority, Luther had no right to secede from her. But if, as Luther claimed, she had through apostasy lost her authority, then, it may be asked, From whence did Luther receive his authority? In all this, Luther's actions were indeed logical, but fatal to the claims of modern sectarians who profess to be the ministers of Christ.

Luther was simply the battle-ax of God to hew down the edifice of popery which stood in the way of human progress. The churches, which, under the leadership of Luther, Melanchthon, Zwingle, Calvin, Knox and Henry VIII. of England, separated from Rome received the name of Protestant. And this very name implies that they were merely a protest against Rome, her teachings and authority. The right of protesting being once granted, it follows that others, also, have the right to protest against them. This principle caused the long and bloody wars which were only closed by the peace of Westphalia, in 1648, and then it was found that central and northern Europe had cast off the intellectual tyranny of Rome, and had established the right of every man to think for himself.

The Protestant party having thus established its existence, by protest and separation, was obliged to submit to the operation of the same principles. A decomposition into many rival sects was inevitable. These having no central or controlling authority, and no longer in fear of their great Roman adversary, commenced bitter warfares on each other; Lutherans persecuted Catholics and Catholics persecuted Protestants, and they in turn persecuted Puritans. Even Calvin proved the darkness of his own mind when he put to death the celebrated philosopher and physician, Michael Servetus, whose greatest crimes were that in religion he denied that the Father, the Son and the Holy Ghost were one and the same person; and in science he had partially succeeded in discovering the circulation of the blood. The circumstances also were of the most atrocious character. For two hours he was roasted in the flames of a slow fire, begging for the love of God that they would put on more wood, or do something to end his torture.

Yet the death of Servetus was not without advantage to the world. Men asked with amazement and indignation if the atrocities of the Inquisition were again to be revived. They saw at once that intolerance was not confined to the Romish church.

In spite of all these commotions, science was making rapid progress. Copernicus lived at the same time as Luther and died two years before him. His was as brave a life as ever lived in story. For thirty-six years—at the very time the Protestant struggle was raging—he was working at that immortal book, in which he so clearly demonstrates the motions of the earth and the revolutions of the planets around the sun. But he did not dare to publish it until there was a lull in the political storm. He was then an old man in broken health. His book was in the printer's hands when he was on his death bed. He waited at death's door from day to day. At length the messenger arrived with the printed book. He received it with tears in his eyes, composed himself and died.

Copernicus was followed by Tycho Brahe, Kepler and Galileo, and last, but by no means least, Isaac Newton, that scientific giant, who burst through the fetters of the ages, and taught man the laws, harmony and grandeur of the Creator's works.

During these troublous times Leonardo da Vinci wrote his celebrated works on mathematics and natural philosophy; and the arts of painting, sculpture and music were greatly improved under the direction of Titian, Corregio, Michael Angelo and Filippo Neri. A few years later Bruno wrote his work on the plurality of worlds.

Copernicus having died soon after the publication of his works, was beyond the reach of his persecutors. Galileo was brought before the Inquisition, and after years of imprisonment, only saved his life by denying the great truths he had discovered. But Bruno heroically refused to recant, and was tortured to death February 16th, 1700, a martyr to the cause of truth.

While these things were transpiring, great changes had taken place in the maratime and commercial affairs of the world. Bold navigators had sailed along the whole eastern coast of America, and a large part of the western coast. Tolerably accurate maps of the outlines of the western hemisphere, had been published as early as 1590. After these discoveries, the great centers of commerce were no longer to be found on the shores of the Mediterranean, but had shifted to the shores of the Atlantic.

England by her geographical position, betwixt the two continents, and in the very center of the inhabitable portion of the earth, as well as the indomitable energy of her sons, had rapidly become the foremost commercial nation of the world.

The great naval armament called the Invincible Armada, was equipped for the subjugation of England; but in the providence of God she destroyed the Armada and paralized the influence of Spain.

In May, 1588, a Spanish fleet of one hundred and thirty ships sailed from the harbor of Lisbon for the English coast. Some of these ships were the largest that had yet been built; they carried eight thousand sailors, and twenty thousand Spanish troops. The pope had blessed the expedition and offered the sovereignty of England as the conqueror's prize. The Catholics throughout Europe were so confident of success

that they named the armament "The Invincible Armada."
So vast was the number of ships that, as they sailed along in
the form of an inverted V (thus $\wedge$), or in the form of a vast
flock of wild geese, the distance from one extremity of the
fleet to the other was more than seven miles.

But they were destined to realize that

> "God moves in a mysterious way,
> His wonders to perform;
> He plants His footsteps in the sea,
> And rides upon the storm."

Scarcely had the fleet entered the English channel when a
storm arose which lasted more than a week.   The wind
blew a perfect gale from the south-west, so that it was impossible for them to return if they had so desired.   The line of
battle could no longer be kept up.   They drifted helplessly
and in disorder up the straits of Dover.   When nearly
opposite Calais, the English loaded several vessels with gun-
power, set them on fire and sent them into the Spanish fleet.
The explosions caused terrible havoc.   The Spanish admiral no
longer thought of victory, but only of escape.   But his dis-
asters were not yet ended.   Many of his vessels were wrecked
on the shores of Norway and Scotland.   In returning around
the north coast of Ireland a second storm was experienced
with almost equal loss.   Only a few shattered vessels of this
mighty armament returned to Spain to bring intelligence of
the calamities that had overwhelmed the rest.   The defeat of
the Armada was regarded even then as the work of Providence.   The Spanish king, when he heard the news, exclaimed,
"I did not expect to fight the elements!"   Thus was the
triumph of the Protestant cause secured, the lovers of freedom
throughout Europe were encouraged, and the power of Spain
forever paralyzed in the affairs of Europe.   Henceforth the
commerce and prosperity of Spain declined.   King Philip,
who had planned the Armada, died in 1598, and bequeathed a
vast debt to his nation whose resources were already exhausted,
notwithstanding her rich mines of gold and silver in the new
world.   In 1589, the next year after the destruction of the
Armada, Henry IV., the first Protestant king of France,

ascended the throne, and by the Edict of Nantes secured to
the Protestants the free exercise of their religion.

England, at that time the mistress of the seas, held
the keys of the commerce of Europe.   Her long con_
flict with her Catholic sovereigns, and the Catholic powers of
Europe, had taught her self-reliance, and had educated her
people in the principles of self-government.   Her laws were
the best the world then new.   Henceforth she became the
favored land of the seed of Abraham, and the asylum of the
oppressed of every nation.

The foregoing will indicate to some extent the condition of
society in Europe at the beginning of the seventeenth century.
It is not surprising that under such circumstances men began
to look toward America, as the land of refuge, where the
institutions of liberty might be planted and fostered, and
political institutions framed which would insure unto all, life,
liberty and religious toleration.

## CHAPTER XI.

### ANCIENT AMERICAN CIVILIZATION.

COLUMBUS DESTROYED PAPAL DOGMAS—CRUELTY OF SPAN-
IARDS—THEIR RETRIBUTION—RELICS IN MASSACHUSETTS
—NEWPORT TOWER—MOUNDS IN OHIO—REMAINS FOUND
IN IOWA—PLATES FOUND IN ILLINOIS—ANCIENT MEXI-
CAN PYRAMIDS—HUMAN SACRIFICES—VIEW FROM THE
GREAT PYRAMID—ANCIENT AMERICAN SCULPTURES—
MAMMOTHS—MEXICAN CUSTOMS—RELIGIOUS RITES—COM-
PUTATION OF TIME—ARTS AND SCIENCES—DESCRIPTION
OF PERU—ITS CIVILIZATION—MASSACRE OF THE INCAS
—TESTIMONY OF TRAVELERS—INDIAN TRADITIONS.

IN ancient times, Rome had taught that the earth was flat;
and that the whole habitable world was comprised in the
three divisions of the eastern continent.   To these divisions

were assigned respectively the descendants of Shem, Ham and Japheth, the three sons of Noah.

When America was discovered, these dogmas were obliged to fall. ' If indeed Columbus had, as he supposed, reached the Indies by a westward voyage, then the world was proven to be a vast ball. If on the other hand America was a separate continent, divided from the eastern by a wild waste of waters of many thousand miles in extent, as was shown by the voyage of Magellan, a few years later, then it was found necessary to account for the origin of the inhabitants.

The teachings of Rome were altogether against their being descended from Adam, since none such were mentioned in their scriptures. The protestant sects were too busy in their rivalries, dissensions and civil wars, to give much attention to the subject. The stupendous event recorded in Gen. x. 25, seems to have entirely escaped their notice. Hence they proceeded to act towards the unfortunate inhabitants of ancient America, as though they did not belong to the human race.

The conquest of Mexico and Peru by the Spaniards will ever remain one of "the bloodiest pictures in the book of Time." By millions upon millions, whole races and nations were ruthlessly destroyed. It was one unspeakable outrage, one unutterable ruin, without discrimination of age, sex or character. Those who fell not by the sword, died under the lash in a tropical clime, or perished in the darkness and dampness of the mines. From the fever-stricken coast of Mexico, and the gloom of dense forests in Central America; from hiding places in the clefts of the rocks, and from the eternal snows of the Andes, where there was no witness but the all-seeing eye of God, there went up to Him a cry of human despair.

The Bishop of Chiapa affirms that more than fifteen millions were destroyed in his time. From Mexico and Peru was crushed out a civilization that might have instructed Europe.

What treasures would now be given for a view of that wonderful civilization and people that met the gaze of Cortez and his companions!

Is it for nothing that Spain has been made a hideous skeleton among the nations—a warning spectacle to the world?

Had not her punishment overtaken her, men would have surely said: "There is no retribution; there is no God." She has been the instrument in the hands of Rome of ruining two civilizations: an eastern and a western: and both of the

ANCIENT PERUVIAN RESIDENCE.

seed of Abraham; and in turn she has been ruined thereby herself.

With circumstances of dreadful barbarity, she expelled the Jews and Saracens who had become the children of her soil by a residence of more than seven hundred years, and in America destroyed nations, in some respects more civilized than herself. By expulsion she lost some of her best citizens; and the wealth of Mexico and Peru, induced habits of luxury and effeminacy among the remainder. Her great cities have sunk into insignificance, and towns that once boasted of more than a million inhabitants can now only show a few scanty thousands. Surely the hand of God is visible in the degradation of Spain.

It is not alone the massive ruins of Central America, Yucatan, Peru and Mexico, that astonish the beholder. In almost every part of the western continent may be found the footprints of a mighty race, now vanished from the earth.

In the copper mines on the shores of Lake Superior, have been found the implements of those who worked in those mines many centuries ago. These instruments are made of copper, yet some of them are of so fine a temper that they will turn the edge of the best steel instruments of our times.

A few years ago, in digging down a hill near the town of Fall River, Massachusetts, a mass of earth slid off uncovering a human skull which was found to belong to a human skeleton buried in a sitting posture. When the covering was removed, the astonished workman saw that the trunk of the skeleton was encased in a breastplate of brass. This breastplate was oval in form, about thirteen inches long, ten in width and nearly one-fourth of an inch in thickness. Below the breastplate, and entirely encircling the body, was a belt composed of brass tubes, each four and a half inches in length and one-fourth of an inch in diameter. The poet, Longfellow, has written a poem on this subject with which, no doubt, many of our readers are familiar. The poem commences:

> "Speak, speak thou fearful guest,
> Who, with thy hollow breast,
> Still in rude armor drest,
>     Comest to daunt me."

Not far distant, on the bank of the Taunton river, is the celebrated Dighton Rock, a huge piece of fine-grained granite covered with sculptures and hieroglyphic inscriptions. Both the skeleton and the inscriptions on the rock seem to be of Asiatic origin. The armor is the same as appears in drawings taken from the sculptures found at Palanque, Mexico.

ANCIENT TOWER AT NEWPORT.

Not far from Newport, in the state of Rhode Island, near the sea shore, is a strange tower, which may have been the base for a beacon or light-house.

At Marietta, Ohio, are ancient works that cover an area about three-fourths of a mile long, and half a mile broad. But the most intricate, and perhaps the most extensive, are those in the Licking Valley, near Newark, Ohio, extending over an area of two square miles.

These mounds are evidently the remains of ancient fortifications, as they are invariably situated on a commanding eminence, or by the side of a stream. Many of these mounds have been found to contain skeletons; and the appearance of the bones would seem to point to an antiquity of more than a thousand years.

Curious pottery, known as "coil-made pottery," has been found in the mounds and caves, and at the ruined "pueblos," or ancient villages, in Utah. These vessels seem to have been formed without the aid of a potter's wheel, by coiling bands of clay upon themselves.

Other relics have been discovered in various parts of the continent which throw some light on the mental and social condition of the ancient inhabitants of America. In August, 1875, on an island in the Mississippi river, near the city of Davenport, Iowa, was found a petrified skeleton. But the most singular part of the find came to light in the hardened and petrified straps, bronze buckles and wooden leg which continued the right extremity, that limb having been removed about midway between the hip and knee. This very interesting discovery proves that the arts of manufacturing bronze, and artificial limbs, as well as the art of surgery, were well known among the ancient Americans. These remains were handed over to the Academy of Sciences, and a photograph was taken of the inscription contained on a rock in the vicinity. A copy of this photograph was forwarded to the late Mr. Barfoot, then curator of the Deseret Museum, in Salt Lake City.

On the 16th of April, 1843, in a mound near Kinderhook, Pike county, Illinois, were found *six plates of brass* of a bell shape, each having a hole near the small end, and a ring through them all. The plates were so completely covered with rust, as almost to obliterate the characters inscribed upon each side of them. But after undergoing a chemical process, the inscriptions were brought out plain and distinct.

There were indications that lead to the belief that this mound was the tomb of a family or person of distinction, in ages long gone by; and these plates probably contain the history of a person or people who existed at a time far beyond the memory of the present race. (*For further particulars see appendix to O. Pratt's Works.*)

"In 1815, near Pittsfield, Mass., at a place called *Indian Hill*, was found what appeared to be a black strap about six inches in length and one and a half in breadth, and about the thickness of a leather trace to a harness. On examination it was found to be formed of two pieces of thick raw-hide sewed and made water-tight with the sinews of some animal and gummed over; and in the fold were contained pieces of parchment, of a dark-yellow hue and on which ¦was some kind of writing. Three of the pieces were preserved and sent to the University of Cambridge, Mass., where they were examined and discovered to have been written with a pen in *Hebrew*, plain and legible. The writing was quotations from the Old Testament, Deut. vi. 4-9, inclusive, and chap. xi. 13-21, inclusive, and Exodus xiii, 11-16, inclusive. (*See Voice of Warning.*)

The ancient Mexican pyramids, "teocallis," or temples of the sun, were still more remarkable. Two of the most ancient of these, near the city of Mexico, were each nearly 200 feet high, and the larger of these two, covers an area of eleven acres, which is nearly equal to that of the pyramid of Cheops, in Egypt.

But the greatest pyramid was that of Cholula. Each side of its base was one thousand four hundred and twenty-three feet, twice as long as the great pyramid of Cheops. It may give some idea of its dimensions to state that its base covers nearly forty-four acres, and the area on its summit embraces more than one. On this elevation stood a costly temple, in which was the image of the mystic deity Quetzalcoatl "god of the air," wearing a mitre on his head, waving with "plumes of fire." A resplendent collar of gold hung around his neck : he held a richly-jeweled scepter of gold in one hand, and a curiously painted shield, emblematic of his rule over the winds, in the other. This temple faced the east, and in front of it, and in view of the whole valley, was the great altar of porphyry on which were offered human sacrifices.

Each year, one was chosen from the most illustrious captives taken in war. He was arrayed in costly apparel. He feasted on the most delicate viands. The people did homage to him as to a king. Whatever could contribute to his pleasure was freely given. At length the fatal day arrives. Slowly and by a circuitous route a procession ascends the pyramid. It is composed of the captive, Mexican priests, and some of the notables of the government, accompanied by bands of music. As they asend the captive throws away his garlands, then his jewels and at length portions of his dress, as emblematic that death will disrobe us all. Having arrived at the top, he is stretched upon the huge altar of stone, and there sacrificed for the sins of the people. Afterwards the people feast upon his flesh—not as famished cannibals—but at a table teeming with delicious fruits and fragrant flowers. They who partook of his flesh were considered to have an especial share in the merits of the sacrifice. Compare with this, John, vi. chapter, 48 to 55 verse, III. Nephi, xviii. chapter. Some idea may thus be gained concerning the origin of these rites and their terrible perversion caused by apostasy.

Nothing can be more grand than the view which meets the eye, from the area on the summit of the pyramid. Towards the West stretched that bold barrier of rocks, which nature has reared around the valley of Mexico. Far away to the East are the barren though beautifully-shaped Sierras, towering high into the clouds and standing like sentinels to guard the entrance to the valley. Three of these are volcanoes, higher than the highest mountain peak in Europe, and shrouded in snows which never melt under the fierce sun of the tropics. At the feet of the spectator lay the sacred city of Cholula with its bright towers and pinnacles sparkling in the sun, reposing amidst gardens and verdant groves.

Such was the magnificent prospect which met the gaze of Cortes and his companions, and may still with slight change, meet that of the modern traveler, as from the platform of the great pyramid, his eye wanders over the fairest portion of the beautiful plateau of Peublo.

Now the question arises, who built these mounds in the Mississippi valley, and these pyramids in Mexico? To what race belong the relics found in Massachusetts, Illinois and Iowa? Surely not to the Indians who were found in America when the country was discovered; for these things indicate a greater skill and culture than those tribes possessed.

Antiquaries have furnished many theories to answer this question which arises in the mind of every student. Some of these theories are very ingenious, but all are lacking in that important element, truth.

For more than three hundred years no certain light was thrown upon the history of that race. But that which man could not find out, with all his learning and research, God has revealed in His own due time. And here we see a wonderful manifestation of the hand of God in the history of this continent. A record, authentic, though brief, has been given to the world. The writings of some of the ancient worthies of that race have been preserved in the earth and have now come forth for the guidance and instruction of living men.

The Book of Mormon contains sketches of their history and the dealings of God with these peoples in a similar manner, as the Bible teaches the history and dealings of God with His ancient people, the Jews. It also contains many incidental references to their mental and social condition and the extent to which the arts and sciences were cultivated among them.

It teaches us that when the Lord confounded the languages at Babel, He led forth a colony from thence to the western continent, now called America. This colony, after crossing the ocean in eight vessels and landing in this country, became in process of time a great nation. They inhabited America about fifteen hundred years but were at length destroyed for their wickedness, about six hundred years before Christ. A prophet by the name of Ether wrote their history and an account of their destruction.

This people is known in modern history by the name of Toltecs, the ruins of whose edifices are widely scattered in Yucatan and Central America.

The sculptures and hieroglyphics on these ruins bear a striking resemblance to those found in the ruins of Babylon and Ninevoh.   It also appears that the mammoth, or American elephant, and mastodon—animals which are now extinct —then roamed the wilds of the western continent; for representations of these animals are often found sculptured on the walls of Toltec ruins.   Some persons have tried to throw

MAMMOTH.

doubts upon these statements alleging that no such animals ever existed outside of tropical regions.   However, numerous remains of them have been found in various parts of America, especially in Kentucky, Ohio, Missouri and Oregon.   In Siberia they have been found frozen in a complete state of preservation.   The illustrious Rufin Piotrowski, a Polish exile, gives a full account of these animals and the methods employed by the Russian government in cutting them out of the ice. (*See Souvenirs d'un Siberien.*)

It is no doubt to these animals that reference is made in the fourth chapter of the book of Ether.

After this, another colony came from Jerusalem about six hundred years before Christ and re-peopled America. This last colony grew and multiplied, and finally gave rise to two mighty nations. One of these was called Nephites, the other Lamanites.

The Nephites were a civilized and enlightened people. For nearly one thousand years they were, from time to time, favored with revelations from God. Prophet after prophet was raised up from among them, and at length they were blessed with a personal appearance of Jesus Christ, after His resurrection, from whose mouth they received the doctrine of the gospel and a knowledge of the future down through all succeeding ages. But, after all the blessings and privileges conferred upon them, they fell into great wickedness in the third and fourth centuries of the Christian era, and finally were destroyed by their enemies, the Lamanites.

But though the Nephite race has vanished from the earth; still 'the grandeur of its ruins attest the greatness of its civilization. Indeed it seems impossible to understand the character and extent of these ruins unless we admit the truth of the records given by Mosiah, Alma and Nephi, concerning the arts, sciences, mode of warfare, religion and subsequent apostasy and degradation of that people. In fact, as researches continue it becomes more and more evident that ancient American civilization was only a transcript of ancient Jewish and Egyptian architecture, manners, customs and modes of thought. In matters of government, the pomp of their monarchs, the arbitrary power, and the obligation of all to military service present a striking resemblance to the powers and privileges of the kings of ancient Israel. Likewise their religious state was only a reflection of that of Asia. Their worship was an imposing ceremonial. Though the common people had a mythology of many gods, similar to the saint-worship of Rome, yet the higher-cultured classes acknowledged but one almighty Creator.

Marriage was celebrated by religious ceremonies and the laws pertaining thereto bore a striking resemblance to those of ancient Israel. Polygamy was sanctioned, but in practice was generally confined to the wealthy.

The priests administered a rite of baptism to infants and proselytes for the purpose of washing away their sins. They also taught that there are rewards and punishments in a world to come—a paradise for the good, and a hell of darkness for the wicked. But the highest glory and reward was preserved for the noble few who fell in sacrifice or in battle for the cause of right. They went directly in to the presence of the sun, whom they accompanied in his bright progress through the heavens. After a few years these spirits went to animate the clouds and add luster to the glories of the sunset, or were sent to rule over and increase the pure and undying light of the stars. Who does not see in all this the traces of a purer religion, which centuries of apostasy and degradation had not been able to entirely destroy? This is all the more manifest when we consider some of their maxims and forms of prayer. One was: "Bear injuries with humility, God, who sees, will avenge you." Another was: "Clothe the naked and feed the hungry, whatever privations it may cost thee; for remember, *their flesh is like thine and they are men like thee.*" Again: "Impart to us, O Lord, out of Thy great mercy Thy gifts which we are not worthy to receive through our own merits." Also: "O, merciful Lord, *thou who knowest the secrets of all hearts*, let Thy forgivness and favor descend." In all these we find sentiments such as are contained in the scriptures of the Old Testament.

One of the most important duties of the priesthood was that of education, to which certain buildings were appropriated. To each of the principal temples, schools were attached and lands were annexed for the maintenance of the priests. Their writings were on cotton cloth or skins, or on papyrus, a kind of paper made from the aloe. At the time of the Spanish conquest, vast collections of these manuscripts were in existence; but the first archbishop of Mexico, burned them in the market-place. Rome was determined that no literature should exist but her own.

The Mexican year consisted of eighteen months and each month of twenty days; five days were added to make the number to three hundred and sixty-five. To provide for the leap years they added twenty-four days to each century. The Mexican mode of reckoning was then superior to that of Europe. When the nations of Europe adopted the calendar discovered and perfected by the Jews and Saracens, then their mode of reckoning corresponded with that discovered by the seed of Abraham on this continent and both were true.

The ancient Americans had ascertained the globular form of the earth previous to their contact with Europeans. Catholic Europe would not admit that truth till compelled to by the voyages of Columbus and Magellan.

Their agriculture was in some respects superior to that of Europe. There was nothing in the old world to compare with the menageries and botanical gardens of Huax-tepec, Chapultepec and Tezcuco.

They excelled in the arts of the jeweller and enameller. They were skillful weavers of fine cloth. They were not ignorant of the use of iron; and understood the manufacture of bronze, of which they also made use. To them we are indebted for tobacco, snuff, chocolate and cochineal. From them we learned the use of the potato, which has now extended to all parts of the civilized world. They, like us, knew the use of intoxicating drinks; and like us sometimes partook of them to excess.

This sketch would be incomplete without a reference to the civilization of Peru. As Egypt was the cradle of civilization in the old world, so Peru was in the new. Like Egypt also it was in most parts a rainless region. The ancient Peruvian empire was nearly two thousand four hundred miles in length, but scarcely sixty miles in width—a narrow strip hemmed in between the grand Andes mountains and the Pacific ocean.

The sides of this great mountain range might seem altogether unfitted for agriculture. But the advanced state of Peruvian civilization is at once demonstrated when it is said that these mountain slopes had become a garden. Immense terraces

wcre constructed wherever required, and irrigation was
employed on the grandest scale the world has ever seen.    Peru
possessed a varied climate.    In the lower valleys near the coast
could be raised all the products of tropical regions, at an
elevation of a few thousand feet the climate was adapted for

MUMMY.

grains of a temperate zone.    On table-lands, at a great elevation above the sea, there were villages and even cities.    Thus
the plain on which Quito stands, under the equator, is nearly
en thousand feet high, and enjoys a climate of perpetual

spring.   So great was their industry that the Peruvians had gardens and orchards above the clouds, and on ranges still higher flocks of sheep and llamas, in regions bordering on the limit of perpetual snow.

In Cuzco, the metropolis, was the residence of the *inca* or emperor, and the great temple of the sun.

The inca was both temporal prince and ruling priest of their religion.   Though they ostensibly worshiped the sun, yet the higher classes recognized the existence of one almighty, invisible God.

Like the Egyptians, the Peruvians understood the art of embalming the dead.   The mummies of their incas being placed in the vaults beneath the temple of the sun, at Cuzco.

This city contained edifices which excited the amazement of the Spanish adventurers themselves—streets, squares, bridges and fortresses surrounded by turretted walls.   The public walls of Peru as well as Mexico were superior to those of Spain herself.   Two great military roads extended the whole length of the empire—one along the coast, the other along the base of the mountains.   These highways greatly aided the Spaniards in their conquest of the country.

Having gained possession of the country and robbed the inhabitants of their gold, silver and precious stones, they put to death the inca and nobility, and took possession of their residences.

The enormous crime of Spain in destroying this civilization has never been fully appreciated.   In vain the Spaniards excuse their atrocities, on the plea that those nations were savages and permitted human sacrifices.   True, the nations of America sank very low when the light of the gospel was withdrawn; but every candid mind will ask: "Which was the more degraded, papal Europe or apostate America?"   Human sacrifice, however cruel, has nothing in it degrading to its victim.   It may be rather said to ennoble him by devoting him to the gods.   Although so terrible with the Mexicans, it was sometimes voluntarily embraced by them as the most glorious death, and one that opened a sure passage into paradise.

There was no spectacle on the American continent, at which a just man might so deeply blush for his race as that presented in Western Europe when the myrtyr, from whom confession had been wrung by torture, passed to the stake in a sleeveless garment, with flames of fire and pictures of devils painted upon it. Let it be remembered that from A. D. 1481 to 1808, more than three hundred and forty thousand persons had been tortured, and out of these nearly thirty-two thousand burnt.

MASSACRE OF THE INCAS.

Let it also be remembered that the body of man is of less value than the immortal soul, for the redemption of which the agony and death of the Son of God was not too great a price to pay. Let it not be forgotten that at that period the entire authority of Europe was directed to the enslaving of the minds and souls of men and making that noblest creation of heaven a worthless machine.

Everywhere throughout the continet may be found traces of Bible and Nephite history. Humbolt, in his travels, mentions a multitude of native books in which were described all the leading circumstances and history of the deluge, of the fall of man, and the first murder as perpetrated by Cain.

Clavigero, in his history of Mexico, tells of an ancient native manuscript, found at Chiapa, which gives a plain and brief account of the building of the tower of Babel, the confusion of tongues, and the subsequent migration of Votan, or Jotan, (no doubt a corruption of Jared) and his companions to the continent of America.

The Indians of Cuba related to Bernal Diaz, a companion and historian of Columbus, a complete and scarcely corrupted account of the deluge, the intoxication of Noah and Ham's shameful conduct.

Humboldt mentions numerous traditions existing among the natives of Yucatan and Central America concerning a great religious teacher, a wonderful personage, whom they called Quetzalcoatl, and who was a white and bearded man. "Many things are said of him in their books of parchment, and among others, that when he left them he gave them wise laws and maxims, and promised to return and rule over them and renew their happiness." Compare with this the record of Nephi. (*See III. Nephi, chap. ii. to xxviii. inclusive.*)

A tradition of the Wyandott Indians, published by Frederick Falley, of Sandusky, O., in 1823, gives a plain account of the battle of Cumorah. Both Breckenridge and Humboldt conclude that "a great battle took place in the region of the great lakes not later than the year 544 of the Christian era, after which the Aztecs [Lamanites] took possession of the country southward."

The foregoing will indicate to some extent the workings of the hand of God, as manifested in the history of this continent. Volumes might be written on this subject, but enough has been said to awaken inquiry among the honest-in-heart and indicate the treasures contained in the Nephite annals, and corroborated by the ruins of

> "This old, old land, which men call new ;
> This land as old as time is old."

## CHAPTER XII.

## THE COLONIZATION OF ACADIA.

ENGLAND'S DEVELOPMENT—REIGN OF ELIZABETH—INFLU-
ENCE OF THE BIBLE—TYRANNY OF THE KINGS—JACQUES
CARTIER—DISCOVERY OF THE ST. LAWRENCE—QUEBEC
FOUNDED—ACADIA COLONIZED—TRANSFERRED TO ENG-
LAND—EXTRACTS FROM LONGFELLOW'S POEM—VIRGINIA
SETTLED.

IN previous chapters we have traced the instrumentalities
which God used in the unshackling of the minds of men
from the superstitions of the past, and disciplining them for
the reception of higher truths. We have seen how, amidst
the rage of tyrants and in spite of the opposition of the
powers of evil, society had gradually climbed to a loftier intellectual eminence than that to which she had attained in any
previous age. The time had at length arrived, when, far from
the jarring scenes of Europe's strife, a nation was to come
into existence, earnest in its love of human liberty, and
vigorous in the execution of its purposes—a nation, which
should accomplish some of the mightiest achievements of the
human race; and where, under the benign influences of its
political institutions, and in the Lord's due time, the gospel
should be again revealed and the Kingdom of God set up
among the children of men.

To rightly understand the history and character of an individual, we must know something of his parentage and the circumstances of his early life. Hence to understand the character
of the American people; we must know something of their
great national mother, the people of England.

The defeat of the great Spanish armada delivered England
from the control of continental Europe, and marked a critical
epoch in her development. From that hour England's destiny

was fixed. She was to be the great protestant power. Her sphere of action was to be upon the seas. She was to take a leading part in the new world of the west. The time was coming when her commerce should surpass all the nations of ancient or modern times; but, above all, her language and literature were fast developing, by means of which her laws and influence would effect the remotest nations of the earth. Hitherto England had lagged behind in the intellectual development of Europe. In the single reign of Elizabeth she leaped to the first rank among the nations of the earth; nay more, she was to become the mother of nations. An impression, vague and shadowy indeed, but none the less real, penetrated the minds of the English people, that they were to be the repository of the divine will, and the executor of His purposes —that the blessings and prerogatives of ancient Israel, were to be their inheritance.

Beneath the rough exterior and blunt manners of that age, lay the new sense of a prophetic power—the sense of a divine commission. And who will say that they were wrong, or prove that they were not divinely commissioned to break down the barriers to human progress, and to some extent prepare society for the "dispensation of the fullness of times?"

The English translation of the Bible, became the great rule of life. The whole moral effect which is now produced by the newspaper, the sermon, the lecture and the circulating library was then produced by the Bible alone; and its effect on the national character was simply amazing. Religion was no longer confined to the cloister and cathedral, but became a subject of thought for every individual. The profound meditations that Shakspeare puts into the mouth of Hamlet were but a transcript of the thoughts and feelings of the earnest men of that age, who saw themselves day by day in the theater of a mighty struggle between the powers of light and the powers of darkness—their souls the prize of an eternal conflict between heaven and hell.

It was this phase of thought that gave to the world the sublime conceptions of Milton, the realistic dreams of Bunyan, as well as the stern and solemn character of Oliver Cromwell and his followers; and made these liberty-loving peasants more than a match for the chivalry and iron-clad knights of King Charles I.

Nor was this feeling confined to any one class. It permeated all ranks and conditions, even to the sovereign. Tradition still points out the tree in Hatfield Park, beneath which Elizabeth was sitting when she received the news of her peaceful accession to the throne. She fell on her knees and exclaimed: "It is the Lord's doing, and marvelous in our eyes." To the end of her reign these words remained stamped on the golden coinage of the realm. Through all her long and eventful life, the feeling seems never to have left her, that her preservation and her reign were the issues of a direct interposition of God.

The foregoing may help us to understand the character of the English people at the time they commenced to plant the institutions of liberty on this coutinent. Who can read the thrilling narrative of English history during the sixteenth and seventeenth centuries without acknowledging the hand of God, in moulding the character of the British people?

It was not a pleasant world which the men and women of Europe had to live in during the sixteenth century. Fighting was the constant occupation of the kings of that time; civil wars were also frequent. In these confused strifes men slew their acquaintances and friends as the only method they knew of deciding who was to fill the throne. Feeble commerce was crushed under the iron heel of war. No such thing as security for life and property was expeted. The fields of the husbandman were trodden down by the march of armies. Disbanded or deserted soldiers wandered as lawless men over the country and robbed and murdered at their will. Epidemic diseases of strange type, the result of insufficient and unwholesome food, and the poisonous air of undrained lands and filthy streets destroyed the inhabitants. Under what hardships and miseries the men of the sixteenth century passed their days, it is scarcely possible for us now to conceive.

From the persecutions of the old world they fled to the wilds of the new. The thrilling story of their adventures, though indeed real, sounds more like romance than reality. Unlike the history of eastern nations, which frequently loses itself in

mists of antiquity, the history of the American people begins
at a comparatively recent date. It is less than four hundred
years since Columbus and his companions first saw the western
continent, and less than two hundred and seventy-five years
since the first colony was planted in the territory which formed
the thirteen original states.

Another peculiarity is, that from the very first this land has
been an asylum for the persecuted and oppressed of every
nation.

It was in the beautiful month of May, 1535, that Jacques
Cartier, a bold navigator in the service of the king of France,
sailed along the shores of the gulf of St. Lawrence, stopping
here and there to examine the country and lay out plats for
future settlements. In July he entered the river St Lawrence and sailed on its broad waters, amidst picturesque scenery
in which was realized all his glowing expectations and dreams.
Leaving his vessel at the present site of Quebec, he proceeded
up the river in a small boat, as far as the Indian settlement of
Hochelaga. This place he named Mount Royal. It is now
the magnificent city of Montreal. However, no permanent
settlements were formed, and it was not till 1604 that De Monts,
Champlain and other explorers began to colonize the country,
on the banks of the gulf of St. Lawrence. Quebec was founded
in 1608. The whole region on the south shore of the gulf was
then called Acadia. Its history shows the wonderful influence
kindness exerts, even among the savage tribes of North America.
Poutrincourt, the governor of the colony, caused an immense
banqueting hall to be erected, which ·was well supplied with
deer, moose, bear and all kinds of wild fowl. He made friends
of the Indians and entertained the chiefs at sumptuous feasts.
In the Winter evenings by the blazing pine logs, Champlain
would relate the stories of his wonderful adventures among
the hills, and valleys, and lakes, and streams, and cataracts,
and red men of the west.

At length, by the fortunes of war, this colony was transferred
to England; but its heart was still with France. The English
distrusted its loyalty, and sent an armed force to surprise and
attack it, and carry away the once happy people, and scatter
them throughout their American domains. The Acadians were

crowded into transports, their families were separated, their friendships and attachments broken up, and they were exiled among strangers, never to see each other again. The name of Acadia was blotted out. Most people are familiar with Longfellow's beautiful story of Evangeline. It is now almost the only memorial that remains of the history of that colony.

As a picture of peace and prosperity, contentment and neighborly love, worthy of imitation in this selfish age, a few lines from Longfellow's beautiful peom, may not be out of place:

"There, in the midst of its farms reposed the Acadian village,
Strongly built were the houses with frames of oak and of hemlock;
There, in the tranquil evenings when sunset had faded to twilight,
Softly the church-bell sounded calling the people to worship.
Thus dwelt in love these simple Acadian farmers,
Dwelt in the love of God and of man. Alike they were free from
Fear that reigns with the tyrant, and envy the vice of republics,
Neither locks had they to their doors nor bars to their windows,
But their dwellings were open as day and the hearts of the owners;
There the richest was poor, and the poorest lived in abundance."

Meanwhile attempts at colonizing were going on farther south. The settlement at Jamestown, Virginia, was founded in 1607. The adventures of Captain John Smith, the virtual founder of the colony, are well known to most readers, as well as the romantic story of Pocahontas, the Indian princess. Its early history is a narrative of strife and human suffering. Many of its early inhabitants were scions of nobility, men unused to toil; in some cases they were mere adventurers, actuated by a lust for gold or love of plunder. However, it teaches one important lesson, that noble birth and high-sounding titles are of little account when compared with the plain virtues of industry, honesty, and trust in God—that it is not men of wealth, but men of noble character that are of most importance in founding a commonwealth.

# CHAPTER XIII.

## COLONIZATION OF NEW ENGLAND.

CHARACTER OF THE COLONISTS—THEY LEAVE ENGLAND—
SOJOURN IN HOLLAND—BREWSTER'S PRINTING PRESS—
PURITANS EMBARK FOR AMERICA—THEIR TRUST IN GOD
—ROBINSON'S PROPHECY—PLYMOUTH FOUNDED—SUF-
FERINGS OF THE COLONISTS—CONFLICT IN ENGLAND—
PECULIARITIES OF THE PURITANS—HARVARD COLLEGE
FOUNDED—EXTENT OF SETTLEMENTS—FIRST CONFEDERA-
TION.

> "What constitutes a state?
> Not high-raised battlements or labored mound,
>   Thick wall or moated gate;
> Not cities proud, with spires and turrets crowned,
>   Not bays and broad armed ports
> Where, laughing at the storm, proud navies ride;
>   Not starred and spangled courts
> Where low-browed baseness wafts perfume to pride;
>   No! Men, high-minded men,
> With powers as far above dull brutes endued,
>   In forest, brake or den,
> As beasts excel cold rocks and brambles rude;
>   Men, who their duties know,
> But know their rights; and knowing dare maintain."

THE mind instinctively turns to the colonizing of New England as one of the great landmarks of human history. A
little more than two centuries ago this land was covered with
forests in which roamed various tribes of Indians; and the
rivers, which now give life to so much cheerful industry, flowed
uselessly to the sea. To-day this same land is covered with
cities, towns and villages, gardens, vineyards and orchards,
schools and palaces—a civilization surpassing, in some respects,
that of any other country on the face of the globe.

Whence came the men who wrought these mighty changes?
What were the circumstances that led them to abandon their

country and their kindred, and all the sacred associations that
link man to his native land, to seek homes beyond the stormy
Atlantic, in a wilderness then inhabited only by savage beasts,
and men still more savage; and above all, that trained them in
the principles of self-government and fitted them to become
the founders of a mighty empire?

At that time protestant princes, no more than popish, were
willing that their subjects should think for themselves. James
I. had just ascended the English throne. His was the head of
a fool and the heart of a tyrant. He was determined that
every one of his subjects should observe the rites and ceremonies of the Episcopal church. On the northern border of
Nottinghamshire stands the little town of Scrooby. Here were
some brave and honest people, to whom the ceremonies of the
Episcopal or Established church were an offense. They held
their meetings in secret, at the house of one of their number,
a gentleman named Brewster. They chose Mr. Robinson,
a wise and good man, to be their leader in spiritual things.
But their secret meetings were betrayed to the authorities
and their lives were made bitter by the persecutions that
fell upon them. They resolved to leave their own land and
seek among strangers that freedom which was denied them at
home.

They embarked with all their goods for Holland. But when
the ship was about to sail, soldiers came upon them, plundered
them and drove them on shore. After some weeks in prison
they were suffered to return home. Next Spring they tried
again to escape. This time a good many were on board, and
the others were waiting for the return of the boat, which would
carry them to the ship. Suddenly soldiers on horseback were
seen spurring across the sands. The shipmaster weighed his
anchor and set sail with those whom he had on board. The
soldiers conducted the remainder back to prison. After a time
they were set at liberty. In little groups they made their way
to Holland, and thus they accomplished the first stage of the
tedious journey from the old England to the new. Here they
remained for eleven years, and worked with patient industry
at their various trades. They gained a reputation for honesty
and skill in all their undertakings, and thus they found

abundant employment. Mr. Brewster established a printing press and printed books about liberty, which greatly enraged the foolish King James. Meanwhile this little band received additions from time to time, as oppression in England became more intolerable. Still they looked upon themselves as exiles. The language and manners of the Dutch were not pleasing to them. They did not wish to lose their identity. Already their sons and daughters were forming alliances that threatened this result. They therefore determined to go again on a pilgrimage, and seek a home in the wilds of America; where they could dwell apart and found a state, where all should enjoy civil and religious liberty.                                            .

They collected their little funds and procured two vessels, the *Speedwell*, of sixty tons, and the *Mayflower*, of one hundred and eighty. The *Speedwell* was found to be unseaworthy and was abandoned. They had not sufficient funds for all to come at once. Brewster was placed in command of the company, which was composed of "such of the youngest and strongest, as freely offered themselves." A solemn fast was held. "Let us seek God," said they, "a right way for us, and for our little ones, and for all our substance."

On a sunny morning in July, 1620, the pilgrims knelt upon the seashore at Delfthaven, while their pastor, Mr. Robinson, prayed for the success of their journey. Out upon the gleaming sea a little ship lay waiting. Money was wanting and so only one hundred could depart. They left the remainder with tears and fond farewells, to follow when they could. Mr. Robinson dismissed them with counsels which breathed a pure and high-toned wisdom. Some of the words which he then uttered, seemed to have a prophetic import. This will be readily seen from the following extract:

"The Lord has more truth yet to break forth out of His holy word. Luther and Calvin were great and shining lights in their times, yet they penetrated not into the whole counsel of God. I beseech of you, remember it, that you be ready to receive whatever truth shall be made known to you."

Who will attempt to deny that God, through him, spake words pregnant with a meaning that men at that age did not understand?

A prosperous wind soon wafted them across the North sea
and they sighted the coast of England.   After considerable
delay at Southampton, Dartmouth, and Plymouth, the *Mayflower* started early in September on her long and lonely voyage from the old world to the new.   After a boisterous voyage
of sixty-three days they espied land, and in two days more
cast anchor in the harbor of Cape Cod.

How truthful the lines,

> "The heavy clouds hung dark
>   The woods and waters o'er,
> When a band of exiles moored their bark
>   On the wild New England shore!"

It was a bleak-looking and discouraging coast which lay
before them.   Nothing met the eye but low sand-hills, covered
with stunted trees down to the margin of the sea.   At first
no suitable locality for a settlement could be found; but at
length they selected a spot where the soil appeared to be good,
with "delicate springs of water."   On December 22, 1620, the
pilgrims landed—stepping ashore upon a huge bowlder of
granite, which is still preserved as a memorial of that event.
The cold was so excessive that the spray froze upon their
clothes till they resembled men cased in armor.   They had
been badly fed on board the ship, which, together with
exposure, caused sickness to prevail among them.   Every
second day a grave had to be dug in the frozen ground.   The
care of the sick and the burying of the dead, sadly hindered their
work; but the building of their little town went on.   When
Spring arrived there were only fifty survivors, and these were
sadly enfeebled and dispirited.   Upon an eminence beside
their town they erected a structure which served a double purpose.   The upper story was used for a fort, in which were
placed six small cannon.   The lower story served for a meet-
ing-house and school-house.

The pilgrims had already drawn up and signed in the cabin
of the *Mayflower*, a document forming themselves into an
organized government, to which they unanimously promised
obedience.   Under this constitution they elected John Carver
to be their first governor.   It is true they acknowledged King
James, but they left no very large place for his authority.

LANDING OF THE PILGRIMS.

They had experienced what despotism was, and they determined from the first to be a self-governing people. In memory of the hospitalities which they had received at the last English port from which they had sailed, this colony took the name of Plymouth.

The years which followed the settlement of Plymouth was a time through which good men found it bitter to live. Charles I., was upon the throne of England. William Laud, archbishop of Canterbury, was the king's right-hand man for dealing out persecution. Whoever refused to perform the religious ceremonies commanded by Laud was forthwith imprisoned. A Scotch clergyman named Leighton, was publicly whipped, branded on the cheek, had one of his ears cut off and his nostrils slit, for calling Laud's ceremonies the inventions of men. Many others were treated in a similar manner. Meanwhile John Hampden, the incorruptible patriot, was arrested for not paying an unlawful tax. A greater than he—his cousin, Oliver Cromwell—was leading his quiet, rural life at Huntington, not without many anxious and indignant thoughts about the evils of his time. He walked over his fields and along the streams,

"Pondering the solemn miracle of life
As one who, wandering in a starless night,
Feels momently the jar of unseen waves,
And hears the thunder of an unknown sea
Breaking along an unimagined shore.
And as he walked he prayed."

The weary victims of this senseless persecution looked to New England for refuge. The pilgrims wrote to their friends at home; and every letter was read with interest. They had hardships to tell of at first; then they had prosperity and comfort; always they had liberty! Every Summer a few ships were freighted for the settlements. At one time eight ships lay in the Thames, with their passengers on board, when the order was issued, that no one should leave without the king's permission. The soldiers cleared the ships, and the poor emigrants were driven back in despair to endure the miseries from which they were so eager to escape. Among these were Hampden and Cromwell. Well would it have been for the

king if he had let them go!    But God had a work for them
to do.   They were to be the instruments in His hand

"To hurl down wrong from its high seat,
    To the poor and oppressed, firm friends and true."

The details of the long war between the king and the people
we need not here relate.    The result was the death of the
unhappy monarch, and another step forward by the British
people in the principles of self-government.

Meanwhile the settlements in America continued to flourish.
The virgin soil yielded abundant harvests.    From the fleece
of their sheep, and the flax of their fields they made a supply
of clothing.    They felled the timber of their boundless forests,
and built ships and sent away to foreign countries, the timber,
the fish and the furs which were not required at home.

They were a noble people who had thus begun to strike their
roots in the great forests of the west.

Their peculiarities may indeed amuse us ; as for example the
strange names they gave their children.    Many of the boys bore
names in memory of some fortunate circumstance, or historical
event, as "Rejoice in the Lord," "Pillar of Fire," "Strength
of Israel," "Praise God Barebones," etc. ;  while the girls
rejoiced in such names as "Truth," "Temperance," "Patience,"
"Chastity," and "Love the Lord."

We may smile at these things ; yet the most wise of all ages
will admire the purity and earnestness of this people.    They
brought with them the love of learning.    In a very few years
schools began to appear.    Such means as could be afforded
were freely given.    Some tolerably qualified brother was
"entreated to become the schoolmaster."    Soon a law was
passed that every township, containing fifty families, must
have a common school.    Harvard College was established
within fifteen years of the landing.    The founders of New
England were men who had known at home the value of
books.    Brewster carried with him a library of two hundred
and seventy-five volumes, and his was not the largest collection
in the colony.    At that time books were very scarce and
twenty times more costly than they are now.

Twenty-three years after the landing of the pilgrims, the
population of New England had grown to twenty-four thou-

sand. Forty-nine little wooden towns, with their wooden churches, wooden forts and wooden ramparts, were dotted here and there over the land. There were then four separate colonies: Plymouth, Massachusetts, Connecticut and New Haven. For mutual defense and protection these colonies united together and thus formed the first confederation of states on the western continent.

## CHAPTER XIV.

### THE CONFLICT IN THE NETHERLANDS.

DESCRIPTION OF HOLLAND—A LAND OF REFUGE—TYRANNY OF ALVA—THE STRUGGLE FOR INDEPENDENCE—SIEGE OF LEYDEN—THE COUNTRY SUBMERGED—FAMINE IN THE CITY—SPEECH OF THE MAYOR—HEROIC CONDUCT—TRUST IN GOD—STORM RAISES THE WATERS—SPANIARDS RETREAT—LEYDEN IS SAVED—THANKSGIVING—WATERS RETIRE.

IN a previous chapter have been described the circumstances which led to the colonization of Acadia and New England.

While these events were transpiring in old England and New England, others of scarcely less importance were occurring in Holland, or the Netherlands, as it is frequently called, and in its colony of New Netherlands. It is a fact too frequently forgotten, that at least three of the thirteen original states were colonized by Holland. It is true Pennsylvania and Delaware received a few colonists from Sweden and Finland, who had settled there to escape religious persecution; but their dominions in the new world were not of long duration. To Holland and England belong the chief glory of colonizing the lands embraced in the United Colonies of 1776. The country now embraced in the states of New York, New Jersey and

Delaware, received the name of New Netherlands, and like the inhabitants of New England, they were for the most part a religious people.

During the fifteenth and sixteenth centuries Holland had been the refuge of exiles from many lands. When John Huss and Jerome of Prague fell under papal vengeance, many of their followers there found a home. When the fury of persecution was raging against the Waldenses, many of them fled to Holland for protection. After the terrible massacre of the French protestants or Huguenots, as they were called, in 1572, many of them took refuge in the Netherlands. This liberty-loving population was the cause of that deadly hatred manifested toward them by the Duke of Alva. This insatiate monster, during his brief administration, caused more than eighteen thousand persons to perish by the hand of the executioner. His cruelties at length aroused the indignation of the people, and brought about those notable events so well described by the historian, Motley, in his *Rise of the Dutch Republic.* This contest was one of the most memorable in the history of the human race, for in it was clearly shown the wonderful providence of God.

Holland, as is well known, is a low, flat country, so low, in fact, that the inhabitants have been obliged to build dykes, or embankments of earth, along the coast, in order to protect the country from the waters of the ocean during high tides and storms. Were it not for this precaution, Holland would frequently present the appearance of a vast, shallow bay or lake, thickly studded with orchards dwellings and cities half submerged in the water.

At this time Holland was under the dominion of Spain. The tyranny of Alva, the governor, provoked the people to resistance, and King Philip sent an army from Spain to enforce submission. Rather than longer endure this oppression, the brave Hollanders resolved to achieve their independence or perish in the attempt. The fortifications of their country were few, but, in one respect, they held the keys of the ocean. They opened the flood-gates of the dykes and prepared to submerge the country when the first storm should come. Meanwhile the Spaniards were besieging Leyden, and if that city fell, the conquest of the country would inevitably follow. The Hollanders well knew that the ocean would damage their fields and destroy their growing crops, but they preferred the chances of starvation to an indiscriminate massacre.

Leyden was situated twenty miles inland. It was impossible to bring Leyden to the ocean. They prayed that God would aid their efforts to bring the ocean to Leyden. Meantime the besieged city was at its last gasp. At the dawn of each day the brave defenders turned their eyes toward the vanes of the church steeples, that they might ascertain the direction of the wind. So long as an easterly wind prevailed, they felt that they must look in vain for the welcome ocean. Yet, while thus patiently waiting, they were literally starving. Such was the condition of Leyden on the 11th of September, 1574. The commander of the Dutch fleet, Admiral Boisot, had constructed a number of flat boats, by which he hoped to be able to bring provisions and munitions of war to the besieged city. But a week elapsed after the opening of the dykes, and no storm nor high tide had come to force the ocean inland. The flotilla of boats now lay motionless in shallow water, having accomplished less than two miles. Everything wore a gloomy aspect; still the hearts of the patriots were lifted to God in prayer. On the 18th the wind shifted to the north-west, and for three days blew a gale. The waters rose rapidly, and before the second was closed, the flat boats were again afloat. Onward the boats flew before the breeze, and soon arrived at the villages of Zoetermeer and Benthuyzen. A strong force of Spaniards were stationed at each place, but they were astonished to see these brave and liberty-loving men, sailing on a sea, where a few hours before, was dry and solid land. Some of their officers even asked in amazement, "was it true that God and the elements were going to fight against them?" Few things are more appalling to the imagination than the rising ocean tide, when man feels himself within its power. The Spanish soldiers saw the waters deepening and closing around them, and, as it were, devouring the earth beneath their feet, while on the waves rode a flotilla, manned by a liberty-loving and determined race, whose courage was known throughout the world. No wonder the Spaniards were seized with a panic and fled precipitately.

Behind them came the roaring tide; and thousands sank beneath the deepening flood. In a few hours the flotilla had arrived at North Aa, from whence Admiral Boiset sent, on September 28th, a carrier pigeon with a letter of encouragement to the famished inhabitants of Leyden.

As time passed on, the mortality in the city became frightful. Mothers dropped dead in the streets with their dead children in their arms. A terrible plague, engendered by hardships and famine, was sweeping away the people like grass before the the scythe. From six to eight thousand human beings sank before this scourge alone, yet the people resolutely held out—women and men mutually encouraging each other to resist the entrance of the foreign foe—an evil more horrible than pest or famine. The heroism of the Hollanders towered to sublimity. True a few of the faint-hearted one day assailed the mayor of Leyden, the heroic Adrian Van der Werf, with threats and reproaches as he passed through the streets. He stepped to one side and mounted the steps of the church of St. Pancras. There he stood, a tall, haggard, imposing figure, with dark visage, and a tranquil, but commanding eye. He waved his broad-brimmed hat for silence, and then exclaimed: "What would ye, my friends? Why do ye murmur that we do not break our vows and surrender the city to the Spaniards? —a fate more horrible than the agony which she now endures. I tell you, I have made an oath to hold the city, and may God give me strength to keep my oath! I can die but once; whether by your hands, the enemy's, or by the hand of God My own fate is indifferent to me, not so that of the city entrusted to my care. I know that we shall starve if not soon relieved; but starvation is preferable to the dishonored death which is our only alternative. Your menaces move me not; my life is at your disposal, here is my sword, plunge it into my breast, and divide my flesh among you. Take my body to appease your hunger, but expect no surrender, so long as I remain alive."

The words of the firm, old mayor, inspired a new courage in the hearts of those who heard him, and a shout of applause and defiance arose from the famishing, but enthusiastic crowd. After exchanging new vows of fidelity with their magistrate, they left the place and again ascended tower and battlement to watch for the coming fleet.

From the ramparts they hurled renewed defiance at the enemy. "Ye call us rat-eaters and dog-eaters," they cried, "and it is true. So long then, as ye hear dog bark, or cat mew, within the walls of the city, ye may know that it still holds out. And when all has perished but ourselves, be sure that we will each devour our left arms, retaining our right to defend our women, our liberty and our religion, against the foreign tyrant. Should God, in His providence, deny us all relief, even then will we maintain ourselves against your entrance. When the last hour has come, with our own hands we will set fire to the city and perish, men, women and children, together in the flames, rather than suffer our homes to be polluted and our liberties to be crushed."

The Spaniards shouted back derisively: "As well can the prince of Orange pluck down the stars from the sky as' bring the ocean to the walls of Leyden for your relief." But they had forgotten that "prayer moves the arm that moves the world;" that He, whom the winds and seas obey, and who holds the tempests as in the hollow of his hand, had heard the cry of that patient and persecuted people, and was sending the darkness and the storm, to sweep away their enemies as with the besom of destruction.

When the stoutest hearts began to fail, the tempest came again to their relief. A violent gale, on the night of the 1st of October, came storming from the north-west, shifting after a few hours, and then blowing still more violently from the south-west. The waters of the North sea were piled in vast masses upon the southern coast, and then dashed furiously land-ward. The waters rose higher than ever before known, and swept with unobstructed fury across the ruined dykes. The fleet of flat-boats at North Aa, was no longer stranded. At midnight, amidst the storm and darkness, Admiral Boisot gave orders to advance. A few sentinels challenged them as they swept by the village of Zoeterwoude. The answer was a flash from Boisot's cannon, lighting the dark, wild waste of waters. Then came a fierce naval midnight battle. It was a strange spectacle among the branches of those quiet orchards and

chimney stacks of half submerged farm-houses. Swiftly the
fleet sailed on over the waters between Zoeterwoude and
Zwieten. As they approached shallows the sailors dashed into
the sea and literally shouldered the vessels through. These
forts and that of Lammen might have proved serious obstacles,
had not the panic, which had hitherto driven their foes before
the advancing patriots, come again to their relief.

A long procession of lights was seen to flit across the black
face of the waters, in the dead of night. The Spaniards had
fled precipitately along a road which led in a westerly direction
toward the Hague. Their narrow path was rapidly vanishing
in the waves, and hundreds sank in the constantly deepening
flood, to rise no more.

The morning dawned, but all was calm and still around the
city of Leyden. The hand of God which had sent the ocean
and the tempest for her deliverance, had likewise struck her
enemies with terror. The lights which had been seen during
the night, were lanterns of the retreating Spaniards. The succoring fleet sailed victoriously into the city on the morning of
the 3rd of October, 1574. Bread was freely given to the poor
creatures, who for months had tasted no wholesome human
food. When the admiral stepped on shore a procession was
formed consisting of citizens, sailors, soldiers, women and
children. They repaired to the great cathedral; and they who
had been firm in their resistance to an earthly tyrant, now
bowed in humble gratitude before the King of kings. After
prayers the whole, vast congregation, joined in the thanksgiving hymn. Thousands of voices raised the song, but few
were able to carry it to its conclusion, for the universal emotion,
deepened by the music, became too full for utterance. The
hymn was abruptly suspended while the multitude wept like
children.

"On the following day, the 4th of October, the wind shifted
to the north-east, and again blew a tempest. It was as if the
waters, having now done their work, had been rolled back to
the ocean by an Omnipotent hand, for in the course of a few
days the land was bare again, and the work of reconstructing
the dykes commenced."

From this terrible ordeal came out many illustrious characters. Its results tended to civil and religious liberty, as well as the great principle of federal union which has since been carried out to such a wonderful extent. These principles the Dutch emigrants brought with them; and when a few years afterwards their settlements fell into the hands of the English they were already assimilated to the ideas prevailing in the New England colonies.

## CHAPTER XV.

### EARLY COLONIAL HISTORY.

RISE OF QUAKERISM—GEORGE FOX—WILLIAM PENN—FOUNDS PENNSYLVANIA—KINDNESS TO THE INDIANS—PHILADELPHIA FOUNDED—MARYLAND, CAROLINA AND GEORGIA SETTLED—ROGER WILLIAMS—RHODE ISLAND FOUNDED—ITS TOLERATION.

THE history of Pennsylvania as a distinct colony began in 1682. Its founder, William Penn, was the son of Admiral Penn, who had gained many victories for England and enjoyed the favor of the king, as well as of the great statesmen of his time. At this time there was in England a numerous sect called Quakers. Some of their principles were true, and most of them were far in advance of the opinions generally entertained in that age.

The rise of the people called Quakers is one of the memorable events in the history of man. It marks the moment when intellectual freedom was claimed by the people as an inalienable right. The sect had its birth in a period of intense national activity, when zeal for reform was invading all ranks of society, and even subverting the throne. Its creed was summed up in one short phrase, "*The inner light or voice of God in the soul.*" Their leader, George Fox, professed to

have visions from heaven.    Having listened to the revelation
which had been made to his soul, he thirsted for a reform in
every branch of learning.    The physician and the scientist
should quit their strife of unintelligible words and solve the
appearances of nature by an intimate study of the laws of

FOX IN DISCUSSION.

being.    The lawyers should abandon their deceit and seek to
establish justice among men according to the teachings of the
Savior.    And the priests should cease to preach for hire, and
seek God in prayer as the oracle of all truth.

No wonder there was a great commotion. In Lancaster, forty priests appeared against him at once. Nothing could daunt his enthusiasm. When cast into jail among felons, he claimed of the public tribunals a release, only to continue his exertions. If cruelly beaten, or set in the stocks, or ridiculed as mad, he none the less proclaimed the principles of his faith. When driven from the church, he preached in the open air; when refused shelter at a private dwelling or humble tavern, he slept without fear under a haystack.

His fame increased; crowds gathered like flocks of pigeons to hear him. His voice and frame in prayer are described as the most awful and reverent ever felt or seen. His clear convictions and glowing thoughts delivered in plain words made him powerful among the masses and the terror of the priests in public discussions to which he defied the world. By degrees "the hypocrites," as the historian Barclay called them, feared to dispute with him. The simplicity of the truth he uttered and the plainness of his speech found such ready acceptance among the people, "that the priests trembled and scud as he drew near, so that it was a dreadful thing to them when it was told them, 'The man in leathern breeches is come.'"

Far from rejecting Christianity, the Quakers insisted that they alone followed its primitive simplicity. They believed in the unity of truth; that there can be no contradiction between correct reason and revelation; and that the Holy Spirit is the guide that leads into all truth. The Quakers read the Bible not with idolatry but with delight, for in there own souls they had a testimony that it was true. "The scriptures," says Barclay, "are not religion but a record of it; a declaration of the fountain, but not the fountain itself." In reading a record of those times it might appear to one that God was then ready to restore His Priesthood and set up His kingdom on the earth. But mankind were not yet ready nor was there a fit place in all the inhabited countries of the world for its establishment.

The well-known William Penn joined this sect, and by this act greatly provoked his father's displeasure. Like Moses of old he refused the favors and honors of the monarch, choosing

PENN'S TREATY WITH THE INDIANS.

rather to obey what he considered to be the truth than to enjoy all the pomp and pleasures of the world. Space will not permit us to relate the story of his sufferings while an exile from his father's home; how he traveled to and fro on the continent of Europe, from the Weser to the Main, from the Rhine to the Danube, distributing tracts, preaching to princes and to peasants, and rebuking every attempt to enthrall the mind of man. Before he had reached the age of twenty-five, he had thrice suffered unjust imprisonment. To the king's messenger, who asked him to recant, he heroically replied, "*Club-law may make hypocrites, it never can make converts.*" Single handed and alone he plead his cause before the highest courts of England. In vain did wicked men endeavor to construe the laws of England to his injury. After a tedious trial he was at length acquitted, though the jurymen were fined forty marks apiece for not bringing in a verdict of guilty. His constancy called forth the admiration of his father. "Son William," said the dying admiral, "if you and your friends keep to your plain way of preaching and living, you will make an end of the priests."

At the admiral's death, William succeeded to his father's possessions. It deeply grieved him that his Quaker brethren should endure such wrongs as were continually heaped upon them. He, therefore, formed the design of leading them forth to America. The king had owed Penn's father sixteen thousand pounds, nearly equal to eighty thousand dollars of our money. Penn offered to relinquish this claim for a grant of land; and the king readily bestowed upon him a vast region, stretching west from the river Delaware, to which was given the name of Pennsylvania. Here Penn proposed to found a state, free and self-governing. He claimed it to be his highest ambition "to make men as free and happy as they can be." When he arrived, he proclaimed to the people that he wished them to be governed by laws of their own making. He was as good as his word. The people elected their own representatives by whom a constitution was framed, and Penn signed this charter of their liberties.

Penn also dealt justly and kindly with the Indians, and they showed a love for him such as they bestowed on no other Eng-

lishman. Soon after his arrival, he invited the chief men of
the Indian tribes to a conference. The meeting took place
beneath a huge elm-tree. The ancient forest had long given
way to the houses and streets of Philadelphia; but a monument still points out to the stranger the scene of this inter-
view They met, Penn assured them, "on the broad pathway
of good faith and good will. All was to be openness and love."
And Penn meant what he said. Strong in the power of truth
and kindness, he bent the fierce savages of the Delaware tribe
to his will. They vowed to live in love with William Penn and
his children as long as the moon and the sun should endure.
Long years after, aged Indians were accustomed to come from
the distant forests and recount with deep emotion the words
that Penn had spoken to them under the old elm-tree.

The fame of Penn's settlements went abroad in all lands.
An asylum was opened for the good and oppressed of every
nation. Grave and God-fearing men from all the Protestant
countries of Europe sought a home where they might live as
conscience taught them.

> "For here the exiles met from every clime,
> And spoke in friendship every distant tongue;
> Men, from the blood of warring Europe sprung,
> Were but divided by the running brook;
> And happy where no Rhenish trumpet sung,
> The blue-eyed German changed his sword to
> pruning-hook."

The new colony grew apace. During the first year twenty-
two vessels arrived, bringing two thousand persons. In
three years Philadelphia was a town of six hundred houses.

Thus did Penn prove himself a benefactor to his race. May
we not also consider him an instrument in the hands of God
for the execution of His purposes?

Meanwhile Maryland had been colonized by Catholics under
Lord Baltimore, in 1634. The first colonists were exiles who
fled here to escape persecution in their native land. Let it
also be said to their credit that they were the first who
embodied in their laws complete religious toleration.

A few scattering colonists had settled within the boundaries
of the Carolinas as early as 1653, and these colonies also became
a refuge for the Huguenots of France.

Lastly Georgia was colonized, in 1732, by the English phil-
anthrophist James Oglethorpe; and it also became an asylum
and a refuge for the deserving poor.

Had these states been colonized immediately after the
discovery of America, they must inevitably have brought
with them the institutions of Catholic Europe. Such, for
example, as still characterize the civilization of Mexico. Even
had they been colonized a century earlier, the colonists would
not have been disciplined sufficiently in the principles of civil
liberty to have built up free and self-governing states.

Who does not see a divine providence—a marvelous wisdom
in all this?

Though the pilgrims had left their native lands, that they
might enjoy the liberty to worship God in the way which they
deemed right; yet they had not discovered that people who
differed from them were as well entitled to be tolerated as
they themselves were. Simple as it seems there are many to
this day who have not found out that every one is entitled to
think for himself.

One day there stepped ashore at Boston, a young man
named Roger Williams. He was a man of culture and refine-
ment, a lover of truth and justice, a man of rare virtue and
power. He had been an intimate friend of Cromwell and
Milton, in the bright days of the poet's youth. Williams
brought to America what was then considered strange opinions.
Long thought had satisfied him that "in regard to religious
belief and worship man is responsible to God alone."

New England society was not sufficiently advanced to receive
such sentiments. Williams had become minister at Salem where
he was held in high esteem. In time his opinions drew upon
him the unfavorable notice of the authorities; and he was
brought to trial before the general court of Massachusetts.
His townsmen and congregation deserted him. His poor wife
reproached him bitterly for the evil he was bringing on his
family. Still he was firm and continued to testify against the
soul-oppression he saw around him. At length the court
declared him guilty and pronounced against him the sentence
of banishment. All honor to this brave and good man! He,
of all the men of his time, saw most clearly the beauty of

absolute freedom in matters of conscience. He cheerfully left his home and wandered in the wilderness. During the part of one winter he lived with Massasoit, the Indian chief, who befriended him and gave him a grant of land, now included in the state of Rhode Island. Here he laid out a city which he called Providence, in grateful recognition of the power which had guided his steps. To-day it is one of the most beautiful and thrifty cities in the United States.

Roger Williams cherished a very forgiving spirit towards those who sent him into exile. Learning that the Indians were planning the destruction of the Massachusetts colony, he boldly went among the Indians and dissuaded them from their purpose. Thus did this good man put his life in peril for his enemies.

Providence Plantation, as it was called, became a shelter for all who were distressed for conscience sake; and so it has continued to the present time. Rhode Island has no record of persecution in her history. Massachusetts continued to drive out misbelievers. Rhode Island took them in. When Massachusetts was convulsed with supposed witchcraft and the horrors of witch-burning, Rhode Island gave no heed to such delusions. In after years, Roger Williams became the president of the colony which he had founded.

The neighboring states were at that time severely punishing the Quakers with the lash, branding-iron and imprisonment; and they invited Rhode Island to join in the persecution. Mr. Williams replied that he "had no law to punish any man for his belief." He was opposed to the doctrines of the Quakers. In his seventy-third year he rowed thirty miles in an open boat to wage a public debate against them. In this manner, and this only, would he resist the progress of opinions which he deemed pernicious. Thus to the end of his life stood forth this good man's loyalty to the absolute liberty of the human conscience. From the foregoing, we may get some idea of the moral and social condition of England and her colonies during the latter part of the seventeenth century.

# CHAPTER XVI.

## MODERN ENGLAND AND HER COLONIES.

CONDITION OF ENGLISH SOCIETY—MANUFACTURE OF GIN AND RUM—ORIGIN OF METHODISM—ELOQUENCE OF WHITFIELD—JOHN AND CHARLES WESLEY—REMARKABLE TEACHINGS—ROBERT RAIKES—JOHN HOWARD—WILLIAM WILBERFORCE—MECHANICAL INVENTIONS—GROWTH OF AMERICAN FREEDOM—THREE GREAT BATTLES—COOK'S VOYAGES—EXTENSION OF THE ENGLISH LANGUAGE—GREATNESS OF PITT—WASHINGTON'S EARLY LIFE—BENJAMIN FRANKLIN.

"Westward the course of empire takes its way."

FROM the first settling of the North American colonies, the relations between Europe and America were such that every great revolution occurring in the parent country had its due effect in the colonies.

In 1688, just sixty-eight years after the sailing of the pilgrims, another famous departure took place from the coast of Holland. It was that of William, prince of Orange, coming to deliver England from tyranny, and give a new course to English history. A powerful fleet and army sailed with the prince, the wicked and foolish King James fled from the people he had so long misruled, and William, prince of Orange, with Mary his wife, were proclaimed joint king and queen of England.

With the revolution of 1688, a new spirit appears in England. Hitherto English philosophy and literature were almost unknown upon the continent. It was only after the revolution that we hear of foreigners visiting England, learning English and seeking to understand English life and character. Thus on the eve of the eighteenth century English ideas took a great stride forward. The people instead of the king became the virtual rulers of the nation.

The preceding age had done its work. It had given to the world the philosophy of Newton, the literature of Shakspeare, and Addison, Pope and Swift, the political agitation of Cromwell, and the colonization of America. The avenues of knowledge were thus opened to the masses. Even the dullest and most backward minds began to have notions of literature and the discoveries of science. The ancient forms of royalty and chivalry had lost their prestige and stood in the shady background of the past. A new world of citizens henceforth occupies the ground, attracts the gaze, imposes its ideas on the public manners and stamps its image on the minds of men. In 1709 appeared the first newspaper, a sheet as big as a man's hand which the editor did not know how to fill. At the present time there are more than 1,000,000,000 copies of newspapers published in the English language annually, many of which contain more reading matter in a single number than the whole New Testament scriptures. With the increase of intelligence the power of the people began to be felt.

Increased intelligence brought political reforms, and these in turn were followed by a reform in morals and manners. During the reign of the Stuarts the morals of the people had been extremely low. As an illustration might be mentioned the disrespect shown to the clergy. A parish priest was only permitted to dine at the second table, after his superiors (?) had been served. He might fill himself with the beef and cabbage, but did not dare to touch the better dishes until invited to do so by the hostess. A law had been passed during the reign of Charles II., that no clergyman should marry a servant-girl without the consent of her mistress. Most of the prominent statesmen during the previous half century were unbelievers in any form of religion. Such were the irreligious tendencies of the age, that drunkenness and foul talk were considered no reproach to Robert Walpole, prime minister of England. Purity of life was sneered at by the nobility as "out of fashion." For example, Lord Chesterfield, in his letters to his son (which were designed for publication), instructs him in the art of seduction, as part of a polite education.

At the lower end of the social scale lay the masses of the extremely poor. They were ignorant and brutal to a degree which it is hard to conceive. The manufacture of gin and rum had been discovered in 1684; and intemperance overran the nation as a plague. Tavern-keepers, on their sign-boards, invited the people to come and get drunk for a penny. For two pence they might get dead drunk, and have "a place to lie down with no charge for straw." Much of this social degredation was due, without doubt, to the apathy and sloth of the religious teachers.

Such was the condition of society when a remarkable religious revival began in a small knot of Oxford students, whose revolt against the wickedness of the times expressed itself in enthusiastic religious worship and an austere and methodical regularity of life, that gave them the nickname of "Methodists."

Of these students, three soon attracted special attention by their religious fervor and even extravagance. One of these, George Whitfield, became the greatest orator. His voice was soon heard in the wildest and most barbarous corners of the land, among the bleak moors of Northumberland, in the dens of London, and in the dark and gloomy mines of Cornwall. Whitfield's preaching was such as England had never heard before, theatrical, extavagant, sometimes common-place, but winning favor by its earnestness and deep tremulous sympathy for the sins and sorrows of mankind.

He was no common enthusiast who could so eloquently plead the cause of the erring and unfortunate as to draw out the last cent from the cool and calculating Franklin, and command admiration from the fastidious and skeptical Horace Walpole; or who could look down, from the top of a green knoll at Kingswood, on twenty thousand colliers, grimy from the Bristol coal-pits, and see as he preached, the tears making white channels down their blackened cheeks.

On the rough and ignorant masses to whom they spoke, the effects of Whitfield and his co-workers were mighty both for good and ill. Their preaching stirred a passionate hatred in

the hearts of their opponents.    Their lives were often in
danger; they were mobbed, ducked, stoned and smothered
with filth; but the enthusiasm they aroused among their followers was equally intense.

Very important to the cause was Charles Wesley, a student
at Oxford, who came as the sweet singer of the movement.
His hymns expressed the fiery zeal of its converts, in lines so
chaste and beautiful that many of the cultured classes were
numbered among the adherents of the movement.

But most important of all was the elder brother, John
Wesley, an ordained minister of the Church of England, who
by his learning, energy and power of organization gave stab-
ility to the movement.    No man of that age surpassed him in
self-denial and trust in God.    With all his extravagance and
superstition, Wesley's mind was essentially practical and
orderly.    He, beyond most men of his age, saw that he lacked
divine authority to found a church.    Hence to the last he
clung passionately to the Church of England, and looked upon
the sect he had formed as only a lay society or branch in full
communication with the parent church.

For a long time he would not permit his co-workers to
administer the sacrament of the Lord's supper; as he considered they did not possess the requisite authority.    Wesley
saw with wonderful clearness a fact that no one of that age
perceived or, if he did, had not the moral courage to declare.
He perceived the universal as well as the total apostasy of the
so-called Christian church.    In his 94th sermon he says; "The
real cause why the extraordinary gifts of the Holy Ghost were
no longer to be found in the Christian church was *because the
Christians were turned heathens again, and had only a dead
form left.*"    In another place he says: "A string of opinions
is no more Christian faith, than a string of beads is Christian
holiness."    The justifying faith which he considered so essen-
tial and taught so earnestly, implied a personal revelation—an
inward evidence of Christanity.    Thus he unconciously yet
logically taught the insufficiency of the ancient scriptures as a
guide to salvation.    It also implied the need of new and con-
tinuous revelation as necessary for the vitality and growth of
the church.    Wesley continued his labors for upwards of fifty-

two years, traveling and preaching until within a short time of
his death, which occurred in his eighty-eighth year. At the
time of his death, his followers numbered more than one hundred thousand. Now they are estimated at nearly eight millions.

It was the teachings and practices of the Puritans, the
Quakers and the Methodists that gave to England that great
moral impulse which led to the establishment of Sunday

JOHN WESLEY.

schools by Robert Raikes of Gloucester, the reforming of
prisons by John Howard, and the abolition of the slave trade
by William Wilberforce. The ardor and perseverance which
these men showed in behalf of the poor, the wronged and
the afflicted, excited a wave of human sympathy throughout the length and breadth of the civilized world. It is from
this time that may be dated the commencement of charity
schools, foundling hospitals, insane asylums and other institu-

tions of benevolence for which English-speaking people are now so famous.

While the moral and religious movements were in progress, others of a political or scientific nature, were pressing forward with rapid strides.    Amid the tumult of these times, James Brindley was quietly making England a net work of canals. Watt was silently perfecting his invention of the steam-engine and Adam Smith was working out the great problem of political and industrial economy, which has made England and her colonies the leading commercial and manufacturing countries of the world.

Meanwhile John Hargreaves, Richard Arkwright and Samuel Crompton, by their inventions were revolutionizing the art of spinning and weaving.    However, these ingenious devices would have done but little had it not been for the new and inexhaustible labor force of the steam-engine which had then come into general use.    One of the first effects was to develop the iron manufactures of England.    Previous to 1750, England and her colonies imported four-fifths of their iron goods from Sweden: now they produce more than four-fifths of all the iron used in the world.

The influence of the steam-engine and spinning jenney on the civilization of England is beyond human calculation. Mines were developed, manufactories established and the whole national industry so increased that the population of England was twice doubled in less than fifty years.    At the same time agriculture was so improved that one-sixth of the people raised food for the remainder.

While these events were transpiring in England they had their due influence in the colonies.    Europe saw for the first time a state growing up amidst the forests of the west, where religious freedom had become complete.    Religious tolerance had been brought about by strange circumstances—a medley of religious sects such as the world had never seen before. New England was the stronghold of the Puritans.    In some of the southern colonies the Episcopal church was established by law and the bulk of the settlers clung to it.    The Roman Catholics formed a large majority in Maryland.    Pennsylvania was a state of Quakers.    Presbyterians and Baptists fled from persecution to colonize New Jersey ; Lutherans and Moravians from Germany abounded among the settlers of Georgia, and the persecuted Huguenots of France had fled from their native land to the forests of Carolina. In such a chaos of creeds, religious persecution was well nigh impossible.

As there were but few large fortunes among the colonists, so nearly all had the same social standing and privileges. Education was general. It was the proud boast of many of the colonies that every man and woman could read and write.

Such was the condition of the colonies in 1748, when Montesquieu, the wisest and most reflecting statesman of France, declared that a free, prosperous and great people were forming in the forests of America. The hereditary dynasties of the old world were all unconscious of the rapid growth of this power, which was soon to involve them in its new and prevailing influence. The hour of revolution was at hand, promising freedom to conscience and dominion to intelligence. From the fragments of European society—fragments that in some instances had been considered worthless—humanity in the providence of God was building up a self-governing and democratic dominion.

About the middle of the eighteenth century occurred three famous battles which did much to determine the destinies of men for ages to come. The first of these, was the great victory achieved by the English arms on the plains of Plassey, June 23, 1757, which laid the foundation of the empire of British India, an empire which comprises more than one hundred and twenty millions of people. The second was the victory of Rossbach, which determined the re-union of the German states and laid the foundation of the present German empire. The third was the triumph of Wolfe on the plains of Abraham, September 13, 1759, for with it virtually began the history of the United States. France had ever been an enemy whose dread had knit the colonists together and to the mother country, England. By wresting Canada from her grasp and breaking through the line with which France had barred the British colonists from the basin of the Mississippi, Pitt laid the foundation of the great republic of the West.

Hitherto the possessions of France in North America had been twenty times as vast as those of England; henceforth they were destined to dwindle into insignificance and eventually become extinct.

The close of the seven years' war, which ended at the peace of Paris, 1763, was a turning point in the history of the world. England was no longer a mere European power. Her future action lay in a wider sphere than that of Europe. Mistress of North America, the future mistress of India, claiming as her own the empire of the seas, Britain suddenly towered high above rival nations whose interest and position, being on a single continent, doomed them to comparative insignificance in the after history of mankind.

It is this that gives William Pitt so peculiar a position among the statesmen of the world. It was his faith, his daring—shall we not say his inspiration?—that called the English people to a sense of the destiny that lay before them.

With England on one side and her American colonies on the other, the Atlantic was dwindling into a mere strait within the British realms; but beyond it to the westward lay a vast ocean where the British flag was almost unknown. True the Pacific ocean had been discovered by Balboa in 1513, and crossed by Magellan in 1521. Dutch voyagers had discovered that "Great Southern Land," which they had named New Holland and also the northern extremity of New Zealand. But the discoveries had remained unheeded for more than a century.

It was not till 1778 that, under Pitt's direction, Captain Cook was sent into the Pacific ocean on a voyage of discovery. He discovered the Sandwich Islands circumnavigated New Zealand and took possession of Australia, or New Holland, in the name of the English king. The reports which he published of that vast ocean and those far-off islands, of their coral reefs, and palms, and bread-fruit, and gum trees, and kangaroos, and tatooed warriors, awoke an interest in the minds of the English concerning this world of wonders. They saw in all this a vast realm opened for the expansion of the English race, and English civilization.

The extension of the English language over vast territories and populations is without a parallel in the history. of the world.  Fully one-fifth of the surface of the globe and one-fourth of its population are under the dominion of England and the United States.  The English language is now spoken, and English and American literature is read in every zone.

"They spread where Winter piles deep snows on bleak Canadian plains,
And where on green Pacific isles eternal summer reigns.
They glad Acadia's misty coasts, Jamaica's glowing isle,
And bide where gay with early flowers green Texan prairies smile.

"They dwell where Californian brooks wash down their sands of gold,
And track the Frazier's swelling flood thro' sunset valleys rolled;
They're found in Borneo's camphor groves, on shores of fierce Malay,
In valleys washed by Ganges' flood where Ceylon's zephyrs stray.

"Old Albions laws, Columbia's songs rejoice the captive's limbs;
The dark Liberian soothes her child with English cradle hymns,
Tasmanian maids are wooed and won, in gentle Saxon speech.
Australian boys read Crusoe's life, by Sidney's sheltered beach.

"They speak to men so far apart, that while this praise we sing,
Some may rejoice with autumn fruits, others with flowers of spring,
They speak with Shakspeare's searching thoughts and Bryant's lofty mind,
With Alfred's laws and Franklin's lore, to cheer and bless mankind."

Who does not see a marvelous wisdom in all this?  The language thus widely spread was destined to be the medium by which the gospel is to be spread in all the nations of the earth.  Who does not perceive that the statesmanship of Pitt was one of the great instrumentalities for the execution of the divine purposes?  Like all great men, Pitt was in advance of the age in which he lived.  But England could not forget the eminent services of him, who had done so much to promote her greatness.  The ashes of Pitt (now best known as the earl of Chatham) repose in Westminster Abbey, the burial place of

the kings of England. History will declare that among statesmen, few, have left a more stainless, none a more splendid
name.

While these leading events were transpiring around them
two remarkable persons were developing in the American colonies. One of these was George Washington, the other, Benjamin Franklin.

Washington was born in 1732. His father, a gentleman of
good fortune, died when his future illustrious son was only
eleven years of age. Upon Washington's mother devolved the
care of his early education. She was a devout woman, of
excellent sense and deep affections, yet of a temper which could
brook no shadow of insubordination. Under her rule—gentle
and yet strong, George learned obedience and self-control. In
boyhood he gave remarkable promise of those excellencies
which distinguished his mature years. His person was large
and powerful. He was accustomed to labor, which gave him
endurance to perform the work that lay before him. His
education was limited to the common English branches, mathematics and land surveying. In his eighteenth year he was
employed by the government as surveyor of public lands.
Many of his measurements are still on record, and long
experience has established their unvarying accuracy. A massive
intellect and an iron strength of will were given to him, with
a gentle, loving heart, dauntless courage, and loftiness of
purpose. He possessed, in a wonderful degree, clear per-
ceptions of his duty, and a deep insight into the wants of his
time.

While Washington's boyhood was being passed on the banks
of the Potomac, Benjamin Franklin was toiling hard in the
city of Philadelphia to earn an honest livelihood. He edited
a newspaper, bound books, made ink, sold rags, soap and
coffee. He also published the first American almanac. A *fac-
simile* of the title page is given on the next page.

He was a thriving man, but he was not ashamed to convey
along the streets in a wheelbarrow the paper which he bought
for the purpose of his trade. As a boy, he had been studious
and thoughtful. As a man, he was prudent, sagacious and
trustworthy. When he had earned a moderate competency he

# Poor Richard, 1733.

## A N

# Almanack

### For the Year of Chrift

# 1733,

## Being the Firft after LEAP YEAR:

| And makes fince the Creation | Years |
|---|---|
| By the Account of the Eaftern Greeks | 7241 |
| By the Latin Church, when ☉ ent. ♈ | 6932 |
| By the Computation of W W. | 5742 |
| By the Roman Chronology | 5682 |
| By the Jewifh Rabbies | 5494 |

### Wherein is contained

The Lunations, Eclipfes, Judgment of the Weather, Spring Tides, Planets Motions & mutual Afpects, Sun and Moon's Rifing and Setting. Length of Days. Time of High Water, Fairs, Courts, and obfervable Days

Fitted to the Latitude of Forty Degrees and a Meridian of Five Hours Weft from London, but may without fenfible Error ferve all the adjacent Places, even from Newfoundland to South-Carolina.

## By RICHARD SAUNDERS, Philom.

### PHILADELPHIA:

Printed and fold by B. FRANKLIN, at the New Printing. Office near the Market.

BENJAMIN FRANKLIN.

ceased to labor at his business. Henceforth he labored to serve his fellow-men. Philadelphia owes to Franklin her university, her hospital, and her first and greatest library. It was he who discovered the identity of lightning and electricity. Before the revolution he was sent to England to plead the cause of the colonists. During the war he was sent as ambassador to the court of France. At the close of the war he was appointed one of the commissioners to negotiate a treaty of peace between the United States and Great Britain. The last great work of his life was to aid in the forming of the constitution of the United States. He continued in public office till within six months of his death and in public service till within twenty-four days of it.

---

## CHAPTER XVII.

### THE EVE OF REVOLUTION.

GATHERING OF POLITICAL FORCES—GENERAL REVOLUTION —CIVIL REFORMS—DECAY OF OLD INSTITUTIONS—ROSSEAU AND HIS WRITINGS—VOLTAIRE—HOLLAND, A POLITICAL REFUGE—AMERICAN SETTLERS—LINES OF ALBERT B. STREET—GROWTH OF THE COLONIES—LOVE FOR ENGLAND—CAUSES OF REVOLUTION—MANUFACTURES FORBIDDEN—STAMP ACT—TAX ON TEA—PHILADELPHIA CONVENTION—ADDRESS TO THE KING—APPEAL TO ENGLAND—TO CANADA—INCIDENT IN OLD SOUTH CHURCH, BOSTON—PAUL REVERE'S RIDE.

"Freedom, thy brow,
Glorious in beauty though it be, is scarred
With tokens of old wars; thy massive limbs
Are strong with struggling. Power at thee has launched
His bolts, and with his lightnings smitten thee.
They could not quench the light thou hast from heaven."

WHO has failed to observe on a calm summer day the elements of a storm collecting silently, and gradually, until the whole heavens grew dark, and the light of the sun was hid? The calm was changed into a tempest, the lightning flashed, the thunder roared, the clouds piled up

thicker and heavier until at length the storm burst, the rain
fell in torrents deluging the earth and in some cases uprooting
the plants it was designed to nourish and strengthen.

So, too, in the political world the forces gather gradually,
until they have attained sufficient power, and then burst
upon the affrighted nations in all the tumult of a terrible
revolution.

There are few intelligent people in this age but what have a
general idea of the history of the world; yet how comparatively few are there who realize the fact, that in the seventy-
five years which elapsed between 1775 and 1850 the great
majority of civilized nations passed through a great social and
political change.   Among the nations so affected may be mentioned the United States, France, Spain, Portugal, Italy,
Greece, Belgium, Poland, Hungary, Turkey, Mexico, Central
America and nearly all the South American states.   To this
may be added the great commot ons in Russia, Sweden,
Norway, Denmark, Holland, Switzerland and the states of the
German empire caused by the wars of Napoleon. In England,
Ireland and Canada, wars were only averted by civil reforms
and concessions to popular rights.

For Europe this epoch was the result of the struggles of
generations.   At the close of the seven years' war in 1763 the
representatives of even the Catholic powers admitted the
decay of old institutions.   The Catholic monarchies headed
by the pope, in their struggle against Protestantism and free
thought had encountered defeat.   From this great struggle
came forth a principle of all-pervaling energy.   The life-
giving truth of the Reformation was the right of private judgment.   The world was rising up against superstition; the
oppression of industry was passing away.   The use of reason
was no longer considered a crime, but was on the other hand,
considered a duty.   Ideas of the brotherhood of man were
flashing across the minds of leading men.

At this juncture a remarkable political writer made his
appearance,   From the discipleship of Calvin, from the
republic of Geneva, from the abodes of poverty, Jean Jacques
Rosseau came as the advocate of the poor and the oppressed.
Through him the "sons of toil" breathed out their wrongs,

and a new class gained a voice in the world of published
thought.     Though full of weaknesses and jealousies and
betrayed by poverty into shameful deeds, he possessed a deep
and real feeling for humanity.     In an age of skepticism he
solaced the ills of life by trust in God.    Fearlessly questioning
all the grandeurs of the world, he breathed the spirit of revolution into words of flame.   What though the church of Rome
cursed his writings with her ban ; and parliaments burned them
at the gibbet by the hangman's hand!   What though France
drove him from her soil, and the republic of his birth disowned
her son!   What though the wise and noble hooted at his
wildness!   Yet from the woes of the world in which he had
suffered, from the wrongs of the down-trodden which he had
shared, he derived an eloquence that went to the heart of the
masses of Europe.   Beyond most men of his time he saw the
hand of Providence in the history of men.

>"Nor God alone in the still calm we find,
>He mounts the storm and rides upon the wind."

Institutions may crumble and governments fall, but it is
only that they may renew a better youth ; the petals of the
flower wither that fruit may form.   On the banks of the
stream of time not a great deed has been done by a hero, or
monument raised by a nation, but tells the story of human
progress.    Each people that has disappeared, every great
institution that has passed away, has been but a step in the
ladder by which humanity ascends to a higher plane.   The
generations that handed the truth, from rank to rank down
the ages, have themselves become dust; but the light still
increases its ever-burning flame.   From the intelligence that
had been slowly ripening sprang the American revolution.
While Rosseau was putting his burning thoughts in print, and
Voltaire, the prince of scoffers, was hurling his venomed
shafts of sarcasm at the priesthood of the Roman church;
farther north was the little country, Holland, which had already
gained a large share of civil and religious liberty.     Here
thought ranged through the wide domain of speculative
reason ; here the literary fugitive found an asylum, and the
boldest writings, which in other countries were circulated by
stealth, were openly published to the world.

While the learned and thoughtful men of Europe were thinking, the pioneers of America were acting. Nothing could restrain them from peopling the wilderness. To be a land-owner was the ruling passion of the New England man. In general, marriages were early and very fruitful. The sons, as they grew up skilled in the use of the ax and the rifle, would, one after another, move from the old homestead; and, with a wife, a yoke of oxen, a cow and a few necessary implements, build a small hut in the forest and by dint of industry soon win for themselves plenty and independence. The beautiful lines of Albert B. Street well describe the circumstances as well as the character of the men who founded American institutions and moulded the national character:

"His echoing ax the settler swung
  Amid the sea-like solitude,
And rushing, thundering down were flung
  The Titans of the wood.
Loud shrieked the eagle as he dashed
From out his mossy nest, which crashed
  With its supporting bough,
And the first sunlight leaping flashed
  On the wolf's haunt below.

"Rude was the garb, and strong the frame
  Of him who plied his ceaseless toil:
To form the garb, the wild-wood game
  Contributed their spoil;
The soul that warmed that frame disdained
The tinsel gaud and glare, that reigned
  Where men their crowds collect;
The simple fur untrimmed, unstained,
  This forest tamer decked.

"His roof adorned a pleasant spot,
  'Mid the black logs, green glowed the grain,
And fruits and plants the woods knew not
  Bloomed in the sun and rain.
The smoke-wreath curling o'er the dell,
The lowing herds—the tinkling bell,
  All made a landscape strange.
Which was the living chronicle
  Of deeds that wrought the change.

"Humble the lot, yet his the race,
    When liberty sent forth her cry,
Who thronged in conflict's deadliest place
    To fight—to bleed—to die:
Who cumbered Bunker's hight of red.
By hope through weary years were led
    And witnessed Yorktown's sun
Blaze on a nations banner spread—
    A nation's freedom won."

A century and a half had now passed since the first colony
had been planted on American soil. The colonists were fast
ripening into fitness for independence. They had increased
with marvelous rapidity. Europe never ceased to send forth
her needy thousands. America opened wide her hospitable
doors and gave assurance of liberty and comfort to all who
came. The thirteen colonies now contained a population of
about three millions.

Up to the year 1764, the Americans cherished a deep reverence and affection for the mother country. They were
proud to be considered British subjects, and of the lofty place
England held among the nations of the earth. They gloried
in the splendor of her military achievements. They copied her
manners and her fashions. Her language, laws and literature
were as fondly cherished by the colonists as by the English
themselves.

Why was it then that such a marvelous change should take
place in the minds of the American people, during the next
twelve years? In 1764 the colonists loved England as their mother
country. In 1776 they had learned to despise her authority.
They bound themselves, by solemn oaths, to use no article of
English manufacture. They publicly burned the Acts of the
English Parliament. They even killed the king's soldiers and
cast from them forever his authority. By what terrible magic
was this change wrought so swiftly: that three millions of
people should be taught to abhor the country they once loved?

To answer this question rightly we must remember that the
cause of the colonists was one of popular rights against
royal prerogative, that the best and wisest men in England
were in favor of the colonists; that even William Pitt, the

greatest statesman England had ever seen, declared openly in Parliament, "I rejoice that America has resisted."

We must also bear in mind that for many years England had governed her American colonies harshly; and in a spirit of undisguised selfishness, America was ruled not for her own good but for the good of English commerce. The colonists were not allowed to export their products except to England. No foreign ships were permitted to enter colonial ports. Whatever were the exorbitant demands of English manufacturers or merchants, still the colonists were not permitted to buy at a cheaper market. Still more, certain goods, woolen for example, were not allowed to be sent from one colony to another. The manufacture of hats was forbidden, and even the Bible was not allowed to be printed in America.

The colonists had long borne the cost of their own government and defense. But in that age of profuse expenditure on useless wars, the king and nobility of England thought to gather from America's toiling sons the means to pay for their own misrule. The Parliament of England passed a law to tax America. The colonists replied they were willing to vote what moneys the king required of them; but they vehemently denied the right of any assembly, in which they were not represented, to take from them any portion of their property. Another law was also passed requiring a royal stamp to be placed on every legal document. Benjamin Franklin had been sent to England by the colonists. He went to plead their cause before the British government. He told them plainly that the colonists could not submit to such taxation. The act was to come in force on the first of November, 1763. On that day the church bells were tolled, and the people wore the aspect of those on whom some heavy calamity had fallen. Not one of the stamps was ever sold in America. Without stamps mercantile transactions ceased to be binding, notes were not legal, marriages were null. Yet the business of life went on. Men married; they bought; they sold—illegally, because without stamps; but no harm came of it.

England heard with amazement that America refused to obey the law. The great statesman, Pitt, denounced the act,

and, at length, it was repealed. The repeal of the stamp act
only delayed for a little the fast-coming crisis.

It was during this agitation that the colonists first felt the
need of a commercial and political union. The idea of a
general congress of the states was suggested, which soon afterwards met in the city of New York.

The king of England was still determined to tax America,
and soon levied a tax on tea. The people determined they
would drink no more tea rather than pay the tax. One day
ships loaded with taxed tea arrived in Boston harbor. There
was a great commotion ; the men ran together to hold council.
It was Sunday, and the people of Boston were very strict, yet
here was an emergency in the presence of which all ordinary
rules were suspended. The crisis had come at length. If that
tea was landed, it would be sold; it would be used, and American liberty would become a by-word upon the earth.

The brave and liberty-loving Samuel Adams was the leading
man of Boston at that time. He was a man in middle life just
forty-two years of age, of cultivated mind and stainless reputation, a powerful speaker and writer, and a man in whose
sagacity and moderation all men trusted. He resembled
Cromwell in some particulars—his love of liberty, undaunted
courage and trust in God. He was among the first to see that
there was no resting place short of independence. He said:
"Our forefathers were driven from the land of their birth in
the cause of religious liberty. They made themselves homes
in the wilds of America. We have earned a competence and
are self-sustaining. We are free and need no king but God."
The men of Boston felt the power of his resolute spirit and
manfully followed where Samuel Adams led. Several days of
excitement and discussion followed. People flocked in from
the neighboring towns. The time was spent mainly in political
meetings. At Fanueil Hall, in the churches and at the market
place, the rights of the people were discussed. One day a
meeting was held and the excited people continued in hot
debate till the shades of evening fell. At length Samuel
Adams stood up in the dimly lighted church and announced:
"This meeting can do nothing more to save the country."
With a stern shout the meeting broke up. Fifty men dis-

guised as Indians hurried down to the wharf, each man with
a hatchet in his hand.  The crowd followed, and stood on the
shore in silence while the so-called Indians went on board the
ship, broke open the chests of tea and threw them and their
contents into the sea.   No wonder King George was in a rage.
No wonder that he demanded that the guilty parties, if they
could be found, should be sent to England for trial.  The great
statesman, William Pitt, also called the Earl of Chatham,
pleaded for measures of conciliation; but all in vain.  General
Gage with four regiments was sent to Boston.  He threw up
fortifications and lay as in a hostile city.   The colonists
appointed a day of fasting and prayer.  · They knew that their
cause was just.   They looked to Him for protection, who
"holds the nations in the hollow of His hand."  They knew
that He, who had guided them across the rolling deep and
had preserved them in the wilderness, could also protect them
from the rage and avarice of wicked men.   They also formed
themselves into military companies.   They occupied themselves with drill.   They laid up stores of ammunition.   Most
of them had muskets and could use them.  He who had no
musket, now got one.  They hoped that civil war might be
averted, but there was no harm in being ready.   While these
things were going on in Boston, a congress of delegates had
met in Philadelphia and were busy discussing measures in
regard to the troubles that were thickening around them.
Twelve colonies were represented but Georgia, the youngest
and feeblest colony, still paused timidly on the brink of the
perilous enterprise.  Some of the truly great men of America
met in that congress.  Of it the great Earl of Chatham said :
"For genuine sagacity, for singular moderation, for solid wisdom the congress of Philadelphia shines unrivalled."  That
quaint old building where they met became one of the spots
ever dear to the patriot's heart.  Among the famous men
assembled there were George Washington whose massive sense
and copious knowledge attracted attention, and made him a
guiding power, and Patrick Henry, then a young man.
He brought to the council a wisdom beyond his years, and a
fiery eloquence, which, to some of his hearers, seemed almost
more than human.   He had already shown that he was

unfitted for farming or merchandizing. He was now to prove
that he could utter words which would sweep over a continent,
thrill men's hearts like the most sublime strains of music, and
rouse them up to high and noble deeds. There also was
Richard Henry Lee, with his bewitching voice, his ripe
scholarship, and rich stores of historical and political knowledge, which would have graced the highest assemblies of the
old world. Nor should we forget to mention the noble-minded
farmer, John Dickinson, whose published letters had done so
much to form the public sentiment. His enthusiastic love of
England was now overborne by a sense of wrong. And last,
but by no means least, we may place on the list the name of
Benjamin Franklin, the sage philosopher, the practical scientist, the shrewd diplomatist, the incorruptible patriot, the
wise philanthropist. Such were some of the men whom God
raised up to mould the character of the infant nation.

Still they did not wish for separation. They wished to have
their wrongs redressed and continue British subjects. They
drew up a narrative of their wrongs. They implored King
George to remove those grievances. They even addressed the
people of Great Britain, as subjects of the same empire, as
men possessing common sympathies and common interests;
yet they added that "they would not be 'hewers of wood and
drawers of water' to any nation in the world." Had all the
colonists been Englishmen or descendants of Englishmen no
more could have been expected. When we recollect that they
had been gathered from many nations and different climes,
their subserviency to the interests of the British empire is
remarkable. The colonists even appealed to their fellow-
colonists in Canada for aid and sympathy. But Canada,
newly conquered from France, was peopled almost wholly by
Frenchmen. They were strangers to the religious struggles
through which the more southern colonists had passed. And
so from Canada there came no response of sympathy or
help.

King George now determined to reduce the colonists to
obedience. All trade with the colonies was forbidden. No
ship of any nation was permitted to enter American ports or
bring supplies to the settlers in America. In justice to the

English people it should be said, that in those days they had
no control over the government of their country. All this was
managed for them by a few great families. Their allotted
part was to toil hard, pay their taxes, and be silent. If they
had been permitted to speak, their voice would have been on
the side of popular rights. They would have vindicated the
men who asserted the right of self-government—a right which
the great mass of Englishmen were not to enjoy for many a
long year after.

Two incidents occurred about this time which well illustrate
the spirit of the people. It was the Sabbath morning before
the battle of Lexington. The scene of the first is the Old
South Church, itself rich with the mementos of the past. Its
walls are lined with monuments. The burying-ground around
the church is a picturesque spot and was first used about 1660.
The trees interweave their branches above the tombs, and only
pencil-rays of sunlight break the broad, cool shadows of the
spot. The Boston branch of the Winslow family rests here, and
here also sleeps the famous Mary Chilson, who is said to have
been the first to step on shore from the *Mayflower*. She died
in 1679. Here lie the remains of Governor John Winthrop;
Hon. John Philips, the first mayor of the city; Robert Treat
Paine, one of the signers of the Declaration of Independence;
and many others among which should not be forgotten the
name of Paul Revere.

At this church the governor of the colony and other British
government officials usually attended. On this beautiful
April Sabbath morning they had come as usual; and the
happy yet determined people were quietly talking and loiter-
ing among the graves of their ancestors. At length the pastor
came, and they followed him into the church. The hymn they
sang is known as the ninety-fourth psalm. It commences:

"O Lord our God, to whom alone, all vengeance doth belong;
O mighty God, who vengeance ownest, shine forth avenging
      wrong,
Thy folk they break in pieces, Lord, thine heritage oppress,
The widow they and stranger slay, and kill the fatherless."

The pastor's text was Psalms xlvi., 1: "God is our refuge
and strength, a very present help in trouble."

He spoke of the wrongs the colonists had endured, the position they held in regard to posterity, and the responsibility which rested upon them to plant the institutions of liberty for the benefit of future generations.   Warming with his theme, he uttered sentences which caused the hearts of foes to quake and the hearts of friends to glow and burn within them. Standing on the platform of truth and right, he dared to hurl defiance at a tyrant king.

The governor, Berkley, interrupted the speaker, and, calling him a traitor, demanded that he should cease.

Some of the militia of Boston foreseeing the danger of the daring speaker had followed him to the church, and already stood in the vestibule.   Just at that moment the trumpet sounded, the drums beat and the great church-bell rang out its clarion notes calling the citizens to arms.   Such was the spirit of the people that the governor sought in vain to stay their indignation which swept like a flood over the land.  With the Puritans liberty was a part of their religion.

The other incident occurred on the eve of the battle of Lexington.

Early in April 1775, General Gage learned that considerable stores of ammunition were collected at the village of Concord, eighteen miles from Boston, and he determined to capture them.   Late on the night of April 18th, eight hundred soldiers set out on this errand.   The patriots observed that there was something more than ordinary in progress.   Companies of soldiers were massed on Boston common under pretense of learning a new military exercise.

Doctor, afterwards General, Joseph Warren, who fell at Bunker Hill, received notice of the design of the troops, and at once sent Paul Revere to arouse the country.  It was agreed that a signal light should be placed in the tower of the Old North Church to notify the watchers of the direction the troops had taken—one if by land, two if by sea. Paul Revere then rowed across the stream to Charlestown.   He was not a moment too soon.   General Gage heard that his plans were discovered, and orders were at once given that no person should be allowed to leave Boston.   Had these orders been given five minutes sooner, the whole course of the revolution

might have been changed.  As it was Revere reached the
other side in safety.  Having obtained a fleet and sure-footed
steed he stood impatiently watching the belfry tower of the
Old North Church.  Meanwhile Warren, in disguise, wandered
through the darkness and listened with eager ears till he heard
the measured tread of the grenadiers marching down to the
boats.  Then with lantern in hand he climbed up into the
belfry and a gleam of light shone over the dark and silent
city.  Paul Revere sprang into the saddle, but paused a
moment and gazed until a second light gleamed out distinctly
and clearly.  Then

> "A hurry of hoofs in a village street,
> A shape in the moonlight, a bulk in the dark,
> And beneath from the pebbles in passing, a spark
> Struck out by the steed that flies fearless and fleet;
> That was all! And yet thro' the darkness and gloom
> The fate of a nation was riding that night,
> And the spark struck out by the steed in his flight
> Kindled the land into flame with its heat.
> It was twelve by the village clock
> When he crossed the bridge into Medford town. .
> It was one by the village clock
> When he rode into Lexington.
> He saw the gilded weathercock swim
> In the moonlight as he passed,
> And the meeting-house windows blank and bare
> Gaze at him with a spectral glare
> As if they already stood aghast,
> At the bloody work they would look upon.
> You know the rest.  In the books you have read
> How the British regulars fired and fled,
> How the farmers gave them ball for ball,
> From behind each fence and farm-yard wall,
> Chasing the red-coats down the lane,
> Then crossing the fields to emerge again
> Under the trees, at the turn of the road,
> And only pausing to fire and load.
> So through the night rode Paul Revere;
> And so through the night went his cry of alarm
> To every Middlesex village and farm—
> A cry of defiance and not of fear—
> A voice in the darkness, a knock at the door,

A word that shall echo for evermore!
For, borne on the night wind of the past
Through human history to the last
The good shall pray and by faith shall hear
A delivering foot-fall as of that steed
And a midnight message as of Paul Revere."

## CHAPTER XVIII.

### THE BOYS OF '76.

BATTLE OF LEXINGTON—OFFICERS CHOSEN—A YEAR OF
DISCUSSION—DECLARATION OF INDEPENDENCE—SPIRIT
OF ENGLISH NOBILITY—DEFEAT OF AMERICAN FORCES
—SUCCESS AT TRENTON AND PRINCETON—SUFFERINGS AT
VALLEY FORGE—WASHINGTON'S PRAYER—BURGOYNE'S
CAMPAIGN—ARRIVAL OF LA FAYETTE—ARNOLD'S TREA-
SON—ANDRE'S DEATH—SIEGE OF YORKTOWN—CLOSE OF
THE WAR—TREATY OF PEACE—ARMY DISBANDED—
WASHINGTON RESIGNS HIS COMMISSION—CONSTITU-
TIONAL CONVENTION—WASHINGTON ELECTED PRESIDENT
—HIS DEATH—HIS TOMB.

WITH the battle of Lexington the war of the Revolution
may be said. to commence. Henceforth the colonies
were united. Georgia no longer hesitated, but sent her delegates to the continental Congress. Resolutions were unanimously passed to provide for the defense of the country. But
it was not till after the battle of Bunker Hill that the people
favored independence. When the tidings of the battle
arrived, Patrick Henry exclaimed: "This was needed to
rouse the country to action." On the same day Congress
appointed George Washington commander in chief of the
colonial forces. On the day following it elected its four major-

generals. From deference to Massachusetts, for the noble part she had taken, the first of these was Artemas Ward. The second was Charles Lee, the son of an English officer, the third was Philip Schuyler, of New York; the fourth was Israel Putnam, of Connecticut. Thus the country took up arms with only one general officer, who drew to himself the trust and love of the country.

Washington immediately accepted the position and wrote to his brother: "I bid adieu to every kind and domestic ease, and embark on a wide ocean, boundless in its prospect, and in which, perhaps, no safe harbor is to be found."

GEORGE WASHINGTON.

Trumbull, the governor of Connecticut, wrote to him: "Now be strong and very courageous; may the God of the armies of Israel give you wisdom and fortitude and cover your head in the day of battle and danger." To this Washington replied: "The cause of our common country calls us both to an active and dangerous duty; divine Providence, which wisely orders the affairs of men, will enable us to discharge it with fidelity and success."

Such were the sentiments which animated the colonists in June, 1775. A year of discussion and anxiety followed, during

which a remarkable pamphlet was published, entitled,
"Common Sense." The writer, who embodied in words the
vague longing of the people, mixed with crude notions of his
own, was Thomas Paine, the son of an English Quaker, and,
at that time, a little under forty years of age. In after years
he became a profligate and a reviler of the scriptures, yet, at
that time, his writings did much to prepare the American
people for self-government.

However, it was not until June, 1776, that the colonists
gave up the hope of reconciliation. At that time the Assembly
of Virginia issued a famous circular entitled, "The Rights of
Man." The leading principles which it taught were, that
"government ought to be instituted for the benefit of the
people ; that freedom of speech and of the press should never
be interfered with; and that religion can be directed only by
reason and conviction, not by fraud or violence." A month
later, July 4th, 1776, the continental Congress issued THE
DECLARATION OF INDEPENDENCE. And for the support of
this declaration they added: "With a firm reliance on the
protection of DIVINE PROVIDENCE, we mutually pledge to
each other, our lives, our fortunes and our sacred honor."

Thus the youthful nation, as it took its place among the
powers of the world, proclaimed its faith in the truth and
reality and unchangeableness of freedom, virtue and right.
The heart of Jefferson, in writing the declaration, and of Congress in adopting it, beat for all humanity. The assertion of
right was made for all nations and for all coming generations.
It was addressed to all mankind and was destined to make the
circuit of the world. As it passed by the despotic countries
of Europe, and the astonished people read with mingled surprise and joy, that "all men are created equal," and have an
equal right to life, liberty and the pursuit of happiness, they
started as from the sleep of years; like those, who have been
exiles from their native land from childhood, start up when
they suddenly hear the dimly remembered accents of their
mother tongue.

When the news of the declaration of independence reached
England the spirit of the nobility was vehement against the
Americans. Had the decision of the conflict hung on the

strength of armies alone, the colonists could not have gained the victory; but it involved the interests of Europe's toiling millions, and brought into action ideas which had hitherto no opportunity for expression, and forces which until then had no sphere of action. The principles that gave life to the new institutions pervaded history like a prophecy, and seemed like the realizing of the golden age of which the poets dreamed. The most profound thinkers and most intense lovers of the race saw in America's future an opportunity for man's higher development; the spiritual-minded saw in the history and circumstances of America the wonder-working and controlling hand of Providence.

The history of the military campaigns of 1776 and 1777, are too well known to need repetition here. The Americans were beaten in every attack made upon them, from the battle of Bunker Hill, June 17, 1775, to the battle of Fort Mifflin, October 22, 1777. At Cambridge they had no powder, yet their courage and perseverance held out. They lost Long Island, New York, Fort Washington and more than three thousand men. They fled through New Jersey followed by the victorious English. The American army kept on dwindling and shrinking till it comprised scarcely seven thousand men, ill armed, unpaid, ill clad and unfed.

During those two years and four months the only battles, that were precursors of success and gave renewed hope and vigor to the patriot cause, were the brilliant successes at Trenton and Princeton.

It was the night before Christmas. The British lay waiting for the Delaware river to freeze over, that they might again pursue Washington and his little band. Meanwhile the Americans collected all the boats up and down the river for seventy miles. After dark they commenced to cross the river. The night was dark and tempestuous, and the weather so intensely cold that two of the soldiers were frozen to death. Yet amidst the floating ice and gusts of wind they fearlessly rowed across the river. At day-break Christmas morning they attacked the astonished royalists. Three times as many prisoners were taken as the number of the American troops engaged. The Americans then recrossed the river taking the

WASHINGTON CROSSING THE DELAWARE.

prisoners with them. A week later, Washington made another night march and surprised the British at Princeton, capturing prisoners and making good his escape.

These exploits, inconsiderable as they may seem, greatly raised the spirits of the American people. When triumphs like these were possible, under circumstances so discouraging, there was no need to despair.

Though the British advanced on Philadelphia and took possession of it, still there was a feeling of insecurity in the British army. They knew not what moment they might be attacked.

Notwithstanding these successes many of the American officers left the army in disgust. The nation could not pay her soldiers and made no promise of future indemnity. The British had full possession of New York, and were rioting and feasting at Philadelphia. Meanwhile Washington with his little army had retreated to a secluded place among the Pennsylvania hills, which was known by the name of Valley Forge.

As the men moved toward the spot selected for their winter resting-place, they had no clothes to cover their nakedness, blankets to lie on, nor tents to sleep under. For the want of shoes, their marches through frost and snow might be traced by the blood from their feet, and they were almost as often without provisions as with them.

An extract from one of Washington's letters to Congress may not be out of place: "We have this day no less than two thousand eight hundred and ninety-eight men unfit for duty, because they are barefoot or otherwise naked. Our whole strength in continental troops amounts to no more than eight thousand two hundred men. Since the fourth instant, owing to hardships and exposures, our numbers have decreased nearly two thousand men. Numbers are obliged to sit all night by the fires; or sleep on a cold, bleak hill, under frost and snow, without clothes or blankets."

All this time the British soldiers in Philadelphia were well provided for; the officers were living in luxury at the expense of the inhabitants. The days were spent in pastime, the nights in entertainments.

It was at this period of the war—the darkest through which the nation ever passed—that the following incident occurred. It was observed that each day after Washington had visited the hospital tents and administered to the sick whatever necessities or comforts he had in his power to bestow, he retired into the forest at some distance from the camp. Curiosity prompted an individual, named Isaac Pitts, to follow him. There, at the foot of a large tree, with head uncovered, kneeling in the snow, was seen the commander-in-chief of the American armies, engaged in prayer before God. With an anxious and burdened mind—a mind conscious of its need of divine support and consolation—Washington went and rolled those mighty burdens—too heavy for him to bear unaided—upon the arm of Omnipotence. Isaac Pitts related what he had seen and heard, and on a subsequent day at least three persons beheld the venerated "father of his country," at prayer before his God.

It is recorded in Matthew vi., 6: "But thou, when thou prayest, enter into thy closet, and when thou hast shut thy door, pray to thy Father which is in secret; and thy Father, which seeth in secret shall reward thee openly." May we not believe that the high moral courage which dared greater perils than the whistling of bullets; that will of mighty strength which having chosen the right, though unpopular, never deviated from it; that calm self-command, which bore up under the greatest reverses and still preserved its equanimity amidst the taunts of enemies and censure of friends—may we not believe that these things were among the open rewards of secret prayer?

From that time forward success seems to have attended the American arms. Meanwhile the tidings of American heroism and suffering had reached the old world and thrilled the hearts of the lovers of liberty in Europe. Prominent among these was the Marquis de la Fayette, a young French nobleman, then scarcely nineteen years of age, who offered to serve in the American army, without pension or allowance. The king of France dreaded the growth of civil and political liberty; yet he could not withstand the temptation to wreak a terrible vengeance on England for having wrested Canada from his grasp. He sent a fleet and army to America, which greatly aided the cause of Independence. Thus did the rage of wicked men further the designs of Providence.

While Washington was still hemmed in among the hills of Pennsylvania, the British general, Burgoyne, had marched from Canada into the heart of New England. At his approach every man took down his musket from the wall and hurried to the front. Little discipline had they, but a resolute purpose and a sure aim. Difficulties thickened around the fated army.

SCENE OF BURGOYNE'S SURRENDER.

At length, Burgoyne found himself at Saratoga. It was now October. Heavy rains fell. Provisions were growing scanty. Gradually it became evident that the British were surrounded. Night and day a circle of fire encompassed them. Burgoyne called his officers together. There was but one thing to do and it was done. The British army surrendered. Nearly six thousand brave men, in sorrow and in shame, laid down their arms. The men who took them were mere peasants. No two of them were dressed alike. These grotesque American

warriors behaved towards their conquered enemies with true
nobility.   General Gates, the American commander, kept his
men strictly within their lines, that they might not witness the
piling of the British arms.   No taunt was offered, no look of

MEETING PLACE OF ANDRE AND ARNOLD.

disrespect was directed against the fallen.   All were mute
in astonishment and pity.

One of the saddest incidents of the war, was the tragic
fate of Major Andre.   The Americans had a strong fortress
at West Point, on the Hudson river.   The English desired to

obtain this place, as its possession would give them command
of the Hudson river, up which their ships might sail more
than a hundred miles.    But that fort, sitting impregnably on
rocks, two hundred feet above the river, was hard to win.
Benedict Arnold, a proud and ambitious American officer,
was in command of this post. Loving money more than duty,
he determined to sell this fortress to the English. He opened
negotiations with Sir Henry Clinton, then in command of the
English at New York, who sent Major Andre to arrange the
terms of the transfer.

At midnight Major Andre landed from a British ship at a
lonely place, where Arnold awaited him.   Their conference
lasted so long, that it was deemed unsafe for Andre to return
to the ship.  It was determined that the next night he should
attempt, in disguise, to reach New York by land.  The pass
given to him by Arnold, permitted him to go through the
American lines.  His danger might now be considered at an
end, and, under cover of the darkness, he rode cheerfully on
his lonely journey, till he came to a small stream.  Thick
woods on each side made the darkness still more gloomy.
Suddenly three men stepped from among the trees and ordered
him to halt.  Thinking them to be friends, he told them he
was a British officer on very important business.  Alas for
Andre! they were Americans.   Andre was searched, and in
his boots were discovered Arnold's drawings of West Point.
The men knew then that he was a spy.  He vainly offered
them a large sum of money, but the men nobly refused to sell
their liberty and their country for gold.  Andre was tried,
condemned, and, ten days after, executed.

His death caused deep sensation throughout the army and
England.  Men in England began to inquire into the causes
of this terrible, fratricidal war.

While the British general, Clinton, was holding New York,
Lord Cornwallis was fortifying himself in Yorktown, Virginia.
The French fleet sailed for the Chesapeake bay, and Washing-
ton decided to act in concert with the French, and lay siege to
Yorktown.   The bombarding was carried on with extra-
ordinary energy.  In a few days the defenses lay in utter ruins.
Cornwallis determined to evacuate Yorktown and join Clinton

at New York.  One night he began to embark his men in
order to cross the York river and set out on his desperate
march.  A violent storm arose and scattered his boats.  All
hope was now at an end.  In about a fortnight from the
opening of the siege, the British army, eight thousand strong,
laid down its arms.

Well might the colonists rejoice for their long and bitter
struggle was about to close.  Eight years had passed since the
first blood was shed at Lexington.  The representatives of the
English people had learned the causes of the American revolution, and refused to continue the fratricidal war.  The independence of the United States was acknowledged and the
British forces were withdrawn.

On the 30th of November, 1782, a treaty of peace was
signed at Versailles, between the commissioners, Benjamin
Franklin, John Adams and John Jay, appointed by the Congress of the United States and those of Great Britain.  The
treaty was not a compact imposed by force, but a perpetual
settlement of all that had been called in question.  By doing
this act of justice to her former colonies, England rescued her
own liberties from imminent danger, and gave a pledge of
liberty to her other dependencies.  That selfish colonial policy,
which had led to the cruel and unnatural war, was laid aside
forever.  Great Britain was henceforth the mother of nations
—the great colonizing power—destined to found colonies in
every quarter of the globe, and sow the islands of the ocean
with the seeds of freedom.

For the United States, the war which began on Lexington
Green, ended with the independence and possession of a
country, which has increased till it is now thirty times larger
than the parent state.

"The boys of '76" had fought their last battle.  December
4th, 1783, Washington came to disband the army.  Many of
the soldiers had been home by permission.  They now came
to bid farewell to their commander-in-chief, and then return
to their great work of building a nation.  Washington and his
soldiers met for the last time.  No more beating of drums
or roar of cannon; no more weary marches or the clash of
arms.  They had fought side by side, and the memories of

those conflicts could never be effaced. Washington said:
"With a heart full of love and gratitude, I now take leave of
you, most devoutly wishing, that your latter days may be as
prosperous and happy, as your former ones have been glorious
and honorable."

The officers then took his hand. There were tears upon his
cheek, and the officers felt a choking in their throats. They
passed out of doors down to the ferry. Washington stepped
into a boat, took off his hat and waved a farewell. The oars
of the rowers soon bore him from New York to the New
Jersey side.

At noon on the 20th of December, he stood in the old hall
of the state house at Annapolis, in the presence of the Congress, which had called him from his quiet home eight years
before, to take command of the armies of the United States.
Now he was to resign it.

He said: "I commend the interests of our country to the
protection of Almighty God, and those who have the super-
intendence of them to His holy keeping. Having finished
the work assigned me, and bidding an affectionate farewell to
this august body, under whose order I have so long acted, I
here offer my commission and take leave of all employments
of public life."

Thus did Washington gladly return to his home on the
Potomac. The simple grandeur of his character was now
revealed beyond the possibility of misconception. Afterwards
he was twice elected president; yet never abused the trust
reposed in him. There were many who would have made him
king. He trampled on their offer, and went back to his fields
of corn and quiet haunts at Mount Vernon. The grandest
act of his public life was to give up power; the most magnani-
mous deed of his private life, was to liberate his slaves.

During the Revolution most of the states had adopted
written codes or constitutions on which all their civil laws
were based. They were virtually, at that time, thirteen independent states. Congress had but little authority; could not
enforce laws or collect taxes. A general constitution was
needed, which would fuse them into one nationality, and control their conflicting interests.

In 1787, fifty-five delegates met in Philadelphia. They came together to devise means for perpetuating the liberty they had so dearly won. Washington was appointed to preside over the Convention; Thomas Jefferson, Patrick Henry, Alexander Hamilton and many other wise men were there. Benjamin Franklin brought to this—his latest and greatest task—the ripe experience of eighty-two years. There were many perplexing questions to be settled. Some of the states were large, others small: ought the small ones to have equal voice

MOUNT VERNON.

in the government with the large ones? They decided that Congress should consist of a Senate and House of Representatives—two senators from each state, no matter what its size or number of population; but the representatives were to be elected according to population. For four months the delegates discussed the momentous issues that came before them. They sat with closed doors; the world will never know how wise or foolish, how eloquent or angry were their words. At one time it seemed impossible to reconcile their differences. Benjamin Franklin proposed that the blessing of God should be asked upon their labors.   From that time forward, prayer

THE TOMB OF WASHINGTON.

was offered each morning,  and greater unanimity prevailed in counsel.   A spirit of concession was manifest, and a willing- ness to give up their private interests for the general good.

Thus did the Spirit of God act on the hearts of the founders of this nation.

. At length they embodied their labors in a written constitution, which, by a vote of the people, became, in 1789, the supreme law of the land. With few amendments the original constitution remains in full force now, receiving, as it increases in age, the growing reverence of right minded people.

Washington was the first president. He took the oath of office April 30th, 1789, in the presence of a vast multitude. He served eight years, and then retired again to Mount Vernon, where he died in the sixty-eighth year of his age, December 15, 1799. His countrymen mourned him with a sorrow, sincere and deep. Their reverence for him has not diminished with the progress of the years. To this day the steamers, which ply upon the Potomac, strike mournful notes as they sweep past Mount Vernon, where Washington spent the happiest years of his life, and where he now reposes.

---

# CHAPTER XIX.

## PROGRESS OF LIBERTY IN EUROPE.

INFLUENCE OF LA FAYETTE—DESPOTISM IN FRANCE—THE BASTILE—CORRUPTIONS OF THE CHURCH—COMMENCEMENT OF THE REVOLUTION—THE MARSEILLAISE—ITS WONDERFUL INFLUENCE—REIGN OF TERROR—NAPOLEON BONAPARTE — HIS WONDERFUL CAREER — JEWISH SANHEDRIM—FALL OF NAPOLEON—HIS DEATH—PROGRESS OF LIBERTY.

WHEN the war of independence was over La Fayette returned to France. He was the lightning-rod by which the current of republican sentiments flashed from America to Europe. He was the hero of the hour. A man who had helped to set up a republic in America, was a dangerous element for old despotic France to receive into her bosom. With the charm of a great name, immense wealth and boundless popularity to aid him, he everywhere urged that men should be free and self-governing. The influence of La Fayette was soon apparent.

The people of France were living under a government which had come down from the feudal ages. They wished to follow the example of the United States, but how could this be accomplished? The king could do as he pleased—make war, build fleets, tax the people, even send men to prison when charged with no crime, keeping them in prison till they became old and gray-haired, or until death set them free. Of all the gloomy prisons of France, the Bastile was the most horrible. Its dark, deep dungeons were ever dripping with water and alive with vermin. No straggling ray of light ever entered them The floor was covered with mud and slime and the bones of victims who had died of starvation.

Louis XV., king of France was accustomed to sign his name to blank letters and give them to his friends to fill in as they pleased the names of those they wished to punish. One day, the king wanted money, and demanded $120,000 of M. Massot. "I cannot pay it," he replied, "Into the Bastile with him," cried the king, and ordered his goods to be seized. M. Catalan was very rich. The king cast him into the Bastile and he did not get out till he handed over $1,200,000! Madame de Pompadour, the mistress of the king, ruled France, and woe to him who provoked her displeasure! M. Latude, twenty years old, offended her, and the great door of the Bastile closed upon him. The years rolled on, Madame de Pompadour and the king went down to the grave, yet M. Latude was still a prisoner in the Bastile. Thus for sixty years did Louis XV., plunder and imprison the people of France.

The nobility, the priests and the officers of the government paid no taxes, but, on the other hand, received great revenues from the people. They had nothing to do except to eat, drink, attend balls or hunting parties and play cards. They lived in fine castles, and had beautiful parks, gardens and hunting-grounds. The tax collectors came several times a year to the poor man's home, but never to the castle. Of every sixteen dollars produced from the land by the hard-working peasants, the king took four, the priests took four, and the nobleman who owned the land took five, leaving only three for the poor man and his family. Meanwhile Louis XVI. succeeded to the throne.

The church was as corrupt as the king. The priests lived luxuriously on the revenue wrung from the toiling people. They charged the people enormous fees for every service, for baptism, marriage, burial, and masses for the dead. From the cradle to the grave it was one continual extortion.

Such was the condition of the people when La Fayette presented to the National Assembly a Declaration of Rights. It resembled the Declaration of Independence in many particulars, and declared that all men are free and equal. It was on Saturday, July 11th, 1789, that La Fayette presented the Declaration of Rights. Sunday came, and the troops were marching. The king had resolved to disperse the National Assembly, and if the people resisted to mow them down with cannon balls. A great crowd assembled in the Palais Royal Garden. They eagerly asked "What is to be done?" A young man named Camille Desmoulins, sprang upon a table, with a pistol in each hand to defend himself. "To arms! to arms!" he cried, "we must defend ourselves!" He plucked a green leaf and put it in his hat-band, for a plume. The people followed his example. They had no arms, but there were muskets in the great arsenal, called the Hotel des Invalides. They broke it open and armed themselves. The cry rung through the streets, "Down with the Bastile!" They rushed to the gloomy prison and planted their cannon to batter down the gates. The guards in the Bastile were heart and soul with the people. They hung out a white flag, and the prison was surrendered. Then came forth to the light of day the emaciated victims who had been so long immured in its filthy dungeons.

A duke rode to the king's palace at Versailles to tell the news. "It is a revolt," exclaimed the king. The duke replied, "Nay, sire, it is a revolution " The deluge of blood had come. Revengeful men were roaming the streets of Paris murdering the nobles and the clergy. The National Assembly ordered the Bastile to be torn down, and the people levelled it to the ground.

In Strasburg, was a young man named Rouget de l'Isle. One day he was dining with his friend Dietrich, and they talked of liberty and equal rights. After dinner, he went to his chamber, sat down to the clavichord and began to play and sing. His soul was on fire for liberty for France. He seemed to be wrought upon by a higher power. Words came, and with them a strange, wild melody. He did not know which came first. He sang and played, and played and sang, and felt a strange delight. At length his head fell upon his breast: he was asleep. The morning sun was shining in his face when he awoke and the song was still stirring in his heart. He called in his friend Dietrich to hear it, he liked it well, and other friends were called in to hear it. A young lady sat down to the clavichord and played while Rouget de l'Isle sang:

"Ye sons of freedom, wake to glory!
  Hark! hark! what myriads bid you rise!
Your children, wives and grand-sires hoary,
  Behold their tears and hear their cries!

"Shall hateful tyrants, mischief breeding,
  With hireling host, a ruffian band,
While peace and liberty lie bleeding,
  Affright and desolate the land?

"Do you not hear the prisoners moaning?
  Arise ye brave, the sword unsheath,
'Neath tyrants yoke no longer groaning,
  Resolved on liberty or death."

The peculiar genius of the French language, as well as the strange versification of the song, will not permit of an exact translation.

For the benefit of those of our readers who understand the French language we give one of the stanzas as originally written:

"Quoi! des cohortes etrangeres,
  Feraient la loi dans nos foyers,
Quoi! ces phalanges mercenaires
  Terrasseraient nos fiers gueriers.

*Grand Dieu! par des mains enchainees,*
*Nos fronts sous le joug se plieraient,*
*De vils despotes deviendraient,*
*Les maitres de nos destinees.*

In a few hours all Strasburg was singing it. It went from village to village, from city to city, from province to province, and became known as the *Marseillaise*, or national song of France, which above all other songs ever written has stirred the hearts of men. Great events took place. The king of France and his beautiful queen, Maria Antoinette, were beheaded. A republic was started, but was soon overthrown, and the government seized by blood-thirsty villains. More than a million people perished by the guillotine, war, famine and starvation.

The nation waded through a sea of blood. Old things passed away never to return. The internal history of France during a period of two years from the fall of the monarchy, is perhaps the most appalling record, which the annals of the human family present.

Why did not France succeed in establishing a free government? Because all such must be founded on intelligence, virtue, and faith in God and immortality. Out of the revolution came the one man who could restore order to France—Napoleon Bonaparte.

It does not come within the limits of this work to relate the various wars of Napoleon. The French revolution—abortive as it seemed—rendered forever impossible the continuance of the despotism which had heretofore governed Europe. Napoleon, though one of the worst despots, sowed revolutionary principles broad-cast over Europe. His judicial code taught the equality of man before the law. His overthrow of so many princes taught the people to place a lower estimate on the sanctity of crowned heads. His consolidation of the petty German states, awakened the desire for a united Germany and paved the way for its accomplishment. He introduced constitutional government to Italy, Westphalia and Spain. He weakend the temporal power of the pope, and dealt fatal blows at the feudal nobility. His rude assaults shook to its foundations the whole fabric of European despotism, and led the lower orders of the people to entertain new ideas regarding their own rights.

Never before had influences so powerful been brought so widely into operation over vast multitudes of men.

Napoleon, with the exception of Oliver Cromwell, was the first great statesman in Europe to engage in designs for the advantage of the Jews. In 1806, the world heard with amazement that Napoleon had summoned a grand Sanhedrim of the Jews to assemble at Paris. The twelve great questions which Napoleon submitted to the Jewish Rabbies thus assembled and

NAPOLEON BONAPARTE.

the answers which they gave to him, did much to dispel popular prejudice against that people, and prepare the way for their social and material advancement. Some of these questions and answers were of peculiar importance in a religious point of view. From these we learn, that in 1806, among the Jewish people, and among some of the advanced thinkers of that age, marriage was considered null and void unless the ceremony was performed by a person possessing divine authority. Further, that polygamy is taught in the Jewish scriptures, but had been discontinued by the Jews by virtue of a decree of the Synod of Worms, in A. D. 1030. (*For further particulars see "Journal des Debats" pour* 1807. *Milman's History of the Jews, page* 592.)

The influence which Napoleon exerted upon the course of human affairs is without parallel in history. In comparison with these, the conquest of Cæsar and Alexander dwindle into insignificance. Never before had any man inflicted upon his fellows, miseries so appalling; yet did never one man's hand scatter seeds destined to produce a harvest of political change, so vast and so beneficent. To the despots of Europe he was the dreaded apostle of democracy. The amazing events which followed each other in so swift succession in France were watched with profound interest in other lands. The results were quickly apparent. When Napoleon fell, the desire for self-government had silently spread over Europe. The anxiety, which the dethroned monarchs evinced to please their subjects, began to disclose to the people the secret of their own strength.

A congress of delegates from the great powers met in Vienna, in 1814, to restore the thrones to the kings who had been exiled during the wars of Napoleon. They were blind to the lesson which the revolution had taught. They dreamed not of the new forces which had been silently growing strong underneath the tumult and confusion of universal war. Napoleon was at length banished to St. Helena, a rocky island in the South Atlantic, far from any other inhabited land, where he died, May 5th, 1821. Thus darkly closed a career the most brilliant, the most influential, and the most remarkable of modern times.

The power of the people now began to be everywhere felt. In 1820, the American possessions of Spain rose against the despotism under which they had long suffered, and successfully asserted their independence. Insurrections broke out in Spain, Portugal, Naples and Piedmont, and only ended when they obtained constitutional government.

Across the Adriatic, Greece took encouragement from the energy of her neighbors to assert the liberty of which Turkish oppression defrauded her.   Helped by Europe, she succeeded.

THE CITY OF ATHENS.

Athens, once the seat of learning and philosophy, the home of poets, painters and sculptors, the city that once led the world in civilization and art, became the capital of the modern kingdom of Greece.

The influence continued to spread until it effected all the states of western Europe. It turned men's minds everywhere to political thought and discussion. It quickened the hardy mountaineers of Switzerland to reorganize their republican institutions, on the basis of equal rights. The little republic of the

SCENE IN SWITZERLAND.

mountains founded so long ago, in the days of William Tell, started on a new era of prosperity. France, in 1830, once more attempted to throw off the yoke of her ancient kings.

These events may be said to mark the complete political awakening of Europe. Western Europe was now free and self-governing. The long and painful transition from despotism to responsible government was at length accomplished. One hundred and eighty millions of Europeans had risen from a degraded vassalage to the rank and condition of freemen.

---

## CHAPTER XX.

### FORCES OF CIVILIZATION IN THE NINETEENTH CENTURY.

THE GENIUS OF THE AGE—EUROPEAN WARS—AMERICA TRANQUIL—DECLARATION OF WAR—DIVISIONS OF NORTH AMERICA—UNITED STATES—CANADA—MEXICO—AMERI-CAN COMMON SCHOOLS—THEIR INFLUENCE—PROGRESS OF INVENTION—FIRST STEAMBOAT—FIRST LOCOMOTIVE—ELECTRIC TELEGRAPH—IMPROVEMENTS IN PRINTING—SPIRITUAL DARKNESS—THE KINGDOM OF GOD—WANTS OF THE PRESENT AGE—JOSEPH SMITH—HIS TRAGIC DEATH—CONCLUSION.

HUMAN history should be a record of progress—a record of accumulating knowledge and increasing wisdom, of continual advancement from a lower to a higher platform of intelligence and well-being. Each generation should pass on to the next the treasures which it has inherited, beneficially modified by its own experience, and enlarged by the acquisitions which itself has gained.

Sometimes the stream of human development seems to pause and the years seem to roll on without change. Yet this is only apparent. All the while there is a silent accumulation of forces, which at length burst forth in the violent overthrow of evils, which had been endured for generations.

The nineteenth century, has witnessed progress beyond all precedent, for it has beheld the overthrow of the barriers that prevented progress. It has vindicated for all succeeding ages, the right of man to his own unimpeded development. The genius of the age has tended to the abolition of serfdom and slavery, and the up-lifting of the poor, the down-trodden and oppressed. More than at all previous times it has seen the removal of artificial obstacles placed in the path of human progress by the selfishness and ignorance of the strong.

At the opening of the nineteenth century, all Europe was occupied with war. From the North to the shores of the Mediterranean, from the confines of Asia to the Atlantic, men toiled to burn each other's cities, to waste each other's fields, and destroy each other's lives. In some places there was heard the shout of victory, in some the wail of defeat. The first twelve years of the century were spent by America in profound tranquility. She looked from afar with a serene neutrality upon the furious efforts which the European nations were making to compass the ruin of each other.

In process of time, England and France, eagerly bent on mutual harm, adopted measures which nearly destroyed trans-Atlantic commerce. American ships lay in unprofitable idleness; grass grew upon the untrodden wharfs of New York and Philadelphia. Moreover the high-handed British enforced a hateful claim to search American ships and take away any sailors suspected of being British subjects.

These grievances might have been peacefully redressed; but America and England were too angry to be reasonable. James Madison was president at that time. He did not want to go to war, but he desired to be elected president a second time. His friends who were eager for war informed him that unless he declared war he could not be re-elected. With closed doors the bill proposing war was discussed. It was passed in secret session, and on June 19th, 1812, President Madison affixed his signature, and issued a proclamation declaring war against Great Britain. The principal European powers, including England, were then engaged in a mighty struggle against Napoleon. England could spare scarcely three thousand men for the defense of her colonies. The British forces in America were principaly composed of Canadian voluntiers and militia.

Then came a war of mingled success and disaster. The surrender of Detroit, the disaster at Queenston Heights, the victory of Perry, the midnight struggle at Lundy's Lane, the capture of Washington, the terrible havoc at New Orleans— all these are too well known to need repetition here. After two years and a half of mutual injuries, a treaty of peace was signed in which nothing was said about the imprisonment of seamen; but from that day to the present no American citizen has been imprisoned on board a British vessel.

Then came an era of peaceful industrial progress without parallel in the annals of the human family. The forces of modern civilization began to work.

North America was now divided into three great divisions, the United States, Canada and Mexico. For obvious reasons the United States has developed the most rapidly. The dominion of Canada is destined in process of years to become a powerful empire. Its area is more than three million five hundred thousand square miles, which is more than that of the United States, and nearly equal to the whole of Europe, Most of this enormous region proves to be of marvelous fertility, producing in abundance nearly all the grains of temperate regions. Millions of acres are added annually to the area under cultivation. The vast and magnificent region watered by the Saskatchewan and Assiniboine seems destined to become one of the granaries of the world. Quietly and peacefully, the dominion is growing in power and influence. The area of cultivated land is fast extending. Manufactures of all kinds are rapidly multiplying, and in ship-building and commerce she has already outstripped the great republic. In these respects, if considered separate from England, Canada now ranks the fourth power in the world.

Recent developments indicate that Mexico has an important work to do in the economy of God. In the last few years she has made astonishing progress in the arts, sciences and social condition of her people. As an illustration one of her sons, the late President Juarez showed himself to be one of the most remarkable men that has lived on this continent during the present century. The population of North America in 1800, was scarcely more than ten millions, now it approaches seventy millions and increases in a ratio that defies calculation. Already it is the theater of some of the most important events in the world's history, and greater events still await the coming years.

At the time that America commenced to be governed by the first written constitution that the world had ever seen, one of the great questions that was asked by the leading minds of the age as well as by the toiling millions of Europe was: "What will be the future of America, what the forces that will mould and fashion it?" One of these was the common school. Here the future citizens met upon a level. Money and position in society counted nothing; merit won. A boy with a patch on each knee, his jacket in rags, who lived in a cabin, whose breakfast was potato and salt, and whose supper was mush and milk, quite likely stood at the head of the class; whi'e the boy who wore good clothes and whose father was rich, possibly found himself at the foot of the long line of spellers.

From these schools many of the boys made their way through college, became teachers, ministers, lawyers, legislators and governors. The lessons there learned together with the instructions of honest God-fearing parents, laid the foundation of character and made them the pioneers of a new civilization.

The education of the masses multiplied the number of thinkers. As a consequence, mechanical skill and invention is the peculiar growth of the present century and the United States in this regard ranks among the foremost nations of the world.

From the creation of the world down to the middle of the last century, nearly all the work of the world had been done by the muscular labor of men or animals.

But in England and America men were discovering that machinery might be made to do work of human hands. It was not until 1764, that James Watt commenced his wonderful inventions, and ten years more elapsed before his engine was of any practical use.

Meanwhile Hargreaves, Arkwright and Crompton had invented machines for the manufacture of cloth. In America there were lands well adapted for raising cotton, but owing to the difficulty of extricating the seeds from the cotton, but little was used and that little was very expensive.    In 1784, only eight bagfuls of cotton were exported from Savannah to England but when Eli ·Whitney invented the cotton-gin in 1792, a great change took place.    It was seen immediately that the machine would do the work of hundreds of men and a new industry and new product was given to the world. Inconsiderable as these inventions may seem, they changed the clothing material of the English-speaking people throughout the world.    In a few years their costume so changed that they might be looked upon as belonging to a different race and a different civilization.

On August 27th, 1787, while the National convention was at work at Philadelphia framing the constitution they were invited to behold a sight that the world had never seen.    It was John Fitch gliding up stream in the first practical steamboat ever constructed.    In July, 1788, the boat made its first trip from Philadelphia up the river to Burlington—amid the . cheering of crowds and the salvos of artillery.    It continued to make trips during part of two years but never exceeded three miles an hour.    As the machinery was imperfect and the running expensive, it was at length abandoned.

Genius is far-sighted and prophetic.    John Fitch looking into the future saw that the time would come when steamships would traverse the ocean, and glide to and fro upon the great rivers of the West.    He went to Ohio to spend his last days, and when the shadow of death was upon him, he made this request, "Bury me on the banks of the Ohio that I may be where the song of the boatmen and the music of the engines shall enliven the stillness of my resting place."    Twenty years passed away before Fich's idea was realized.    At length Robert Fulton built the Clermont in 1807 and started up the Hudson river. The country people knew not what to make of it.    A Dutchman shouted to his wife, "The devil is on his way up the river with a sawmill in a boat."    Fulton had succeeded where others had failed.    It was the beginning of a new era in navigation. In 1819, the *Savannah* was the first steamboat to cross the Atlantic ocean.    John Stevens of Hoboken, New Jersey appeared in 1812 before Congress with a plan for a railroad,

AN OCEAN STEAMER.

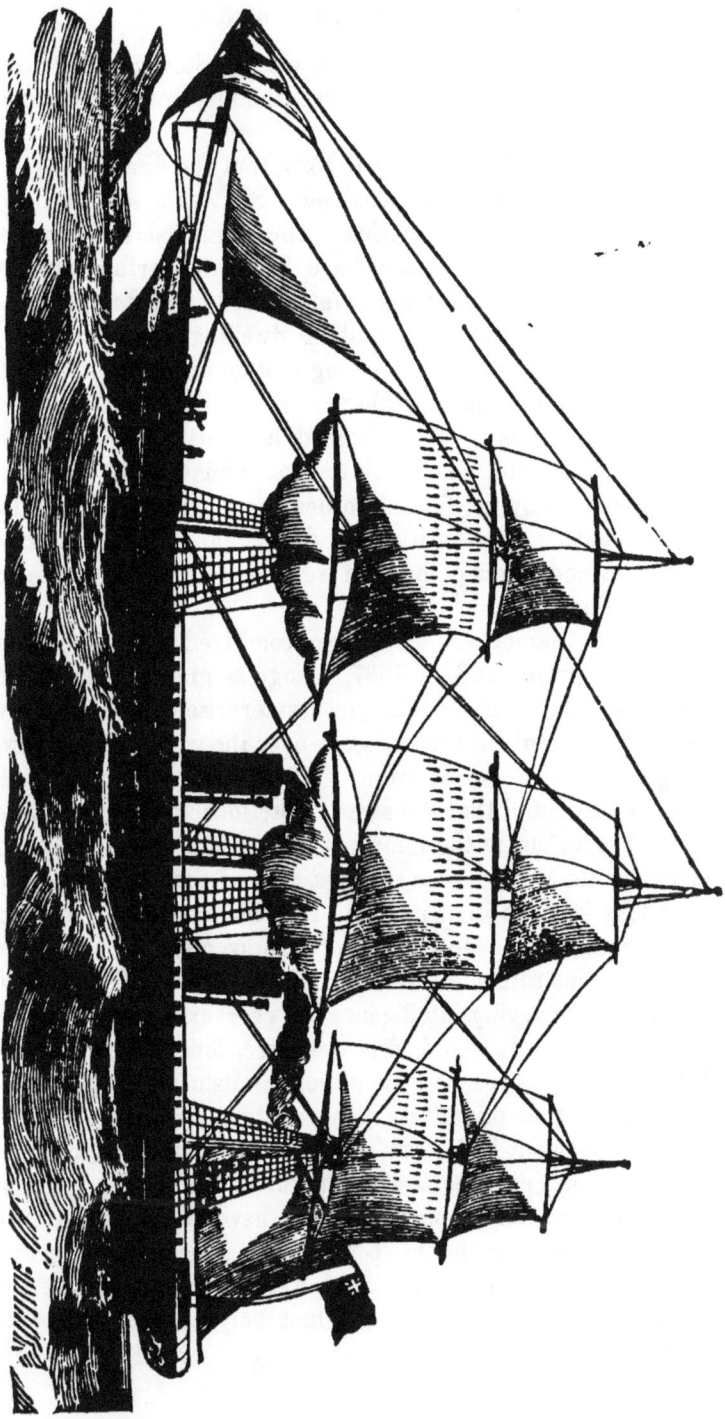

Two years later, July 25th, 1814, George Stevenson of England completed and run the Rocket, the first practical locomotive in the world,

But it was not till September, 1825, that the first railway for passengers was opened in England. Six years later railway trains were running in America. The improved facilities for traveling by means of steam, have had a wonderful influence upon society. A century ago human society was composed of a multitude of little communities, dwelling apart, mutually ignorant, and therefore, cherishing mutual antipathies. Facilities of travel brought together men of different towns and different countries. They learned how little there was, on either side, to hate, how much to love. Thus ancient prejudice was broken up by the fuller knowledge gained by this extended acquaintance. Peculiarities of dialect and manners grew indistinct, and errors of opinion were corrected by friendly conflict of mind.

In 1832, Samuel F. B. Morse, conceived the idea of the electric telegraph, and in 1837, Congress granted him thirty thousand dollars to aid his great enterprise. In 1844, Professor Morse sent his first message over the world's first electric telegraph. The words were, "What hath God wrought!" Thus it was found that the same mysterious and terrible power which flashes out in the midnight storm was ready to convey across continents and seas the messages of man. This use of electricity is of peculiar interest. It is the first invention which is apparently final. In the race of improvement all other inventions and instrumentalities may be superceded. But what agency for conveying intelligence can ever excel that which is instantaneous? It would seem that here, for the first time, the human mind has reached the utmost limits of its progress.

From the time of its first invention to the year 1814, scarcely any improvement had been made on the printing press. A rude machine, printing at its best scarcely 150 copies per hour, was still universally in use. Now we have machines that print 25,000 copies per hour; books and papers have greatly cheapened in consequence. Such were some of the forces at work upon society during the first half of the nineteenth century.

But while mankind had progressed in science they had remained stationary in religion; and how could it be otherwise? Invention and discovery are but the unfolding of the laws, attributes and objects of nature to man's limited understanding —the action of the divine will on the minds of men. When God revealed nature's laws, man progressed scientifically: until God revealed religious truth man groped in spiritual darkness. The intellectual light of that age only made to observing minds, their spiritual night more palpable; even as a candle shining in the night only intensifies the surrounding gloom. Many leading minds perceived somewhat, the errors of the times, and sought to bring about reform in various ways. These attempts brought forth discussion and division. The disintegration which had commenced in the days of Luther, now worked with unexampled rapidity, until the various so-called Christian sects numbered more than six hundred, each tenacious of its own ideas, and bitterly denouncing all the others.

None of these jarring sects ever had divine authority; in fact, they denied the possibility of revelation from God. Even admitting their claims, their creeds are only the crystalized ideas of the leading men of the age that gave them birth. For example, Rome depended not upon revelation, nor even upon the letter of the scriptures, but upon the tradition of the fathers. In other words, the rule of faith, in the church of Rome was the conflicting opinions of men—often ill-informed and superstitious—who lived between the great apostasy and the time of Luther.

So again, the creed of Lutherism is only the best ideas of men who lived in Central Europe three hundred and fifty years ago. In like manner, Presbyterianism is the reflex of the stern and rugged character of the Scotch in the 17th century. So also Methodism and Quakerism are the products of zealous English reformers in the 17th and 18th centuries. All of the religions that existed in America at the beginning of this century, were the outgrowth of European thought. They were systems that had been transplanted from foreign lands, by no means adapted to the progressive ideas that prevail on this continent.

Humanly speaking, it was time to establish a religion, which should harmonize with the circumstances and age in which we live. Divinely speaking, man had become so developed and disciplined that he could receive the gospel. It was the Lord's due time to again reveal His will and set up His kingdom upon the earth.

Not only was the age peculiar, but likewise the land in which this work was to be accomplished. The governments of European countries were all committed to some particular creed, some peculiar form of religious worship. But in America there was no established religion. All were free to accept or reject the truth untrammelled by the arbitrary requirements of the civil law.

The instrumentalities used for the establishment of this work were very peculiar. No hoary-headed philosopher, full of worldly wisdom; no crafty politician, zealous for a party or sect; no profound doctor of divinity, deeply versed in antiquarian lore, was appointed to do this work. No! A pure and ingenuous youth, who had spent the few years of his mortal life in the quiet and peaceful avocations of agricultural life—a youth who had not yet drunk in the poison of man's theology —such was the instrument chosen by the Almighty for the execution of His purposes.

The sublime and tragic history of Joseph Smith is too well known to need repetition here. A few leading facts will suffice. Joseph Smith was born December 23rd, 1805, at Sharon, Windsor Co., Vt. He received his first vision on the morning of a beautiful, clear day, early in the Spring of 1820. Joseph was then a little more than fourteen years of age. Three years and a half passed away, when he received his second vision. It was September 21st, 1823; he had retired to rest when the divine messenger made his appearance. During the night the angel appeared three times to Joseph, and immediately after, the dawn approached; so that their interviews must have occupied the whole of that night. Thrice had the angel descended, and thrice had he ascended, with all the circumstances of reality. There is something grand in the very simplicity of the narrative of Joseph and all the more impressive when we consider his mental and physical characteristics—a man of lofty stature and giant mind. He dwelt in the very glare and illumination of a spiritual existence, and yet was the founder, organizer and leader of a latter-day Israel. Not more real was Jacob's angel with whom he wrestled all night, than were the angels of our times to Joseph. Then he commenced a life of toil and persecution—toil in the service of his divine Master, persecution from the enemy of all good.

We can only understand the life and character of Joseph Smith, when we consider the peculiar wants of the present age. Never was there a time in the history of the race when learning and general intelligence were so well diffused as at the present. The press is throwing off continually its millions of printed pages which are scattered broadcast, as the leaves of autumn.

Never was there a time of more intense activity. Who can pass through the crowded streets of our cities, listen to the throbbing of the steam engine, the hum of machinery, gaze at the vast trains that are driven with fire and vapor along our railways, or view those magnificent structures that cross the mighty deep without feeling that this is an earnest age?

Now this earnest, active, thinking age, demands a religion that has life and power in it. Not a religion of cold formality and narrow sectarianism, but a religion that will satisfy the intelligent with its truths, and touch the heart with its love, and sway the will with its persuasiveness, and gratify the taste with its beauties, and fill the imagination with its sublimities. A religion is wanted that will enlist upon its side the whole nature of man and command his willing and devoted homage; a religion, that, bearing the full impress of its Author's image, shall carry its own credentials with it, and which, clothed with all the elements of truth and righteousness, beauty and grandeur, of love and power, shall be revered by all those who love the truth, and dreaded by all who love it not.

It is evident to every thinking mind that the strife and confusion and babel of the six hundred jarring sects of Christendom can not do this. Their half-deserted cathedrals and cold, formal ceremonies, as well as the triumphant march of infidelity and crime, attest the fact, that they have lost their hold on the masses of men.

As in the days of old the Lord renewed his communications with man through the dutiful and obedient Samuel; so in this age he spake to the youthful Joseph. And how did Joseph accomplish so much in so short a time? Simply because he entered into his work with his whole heart. He allowed no inferior object to weaken his interest or divide his attention, and he continually sought the inspiration of the Almighty, who came to his aid and enabled him to accomplish in the short space of a few years the mightiest work that any man has wrought since the Savior was upon the earth. After an active and self-sacrificing life of nearly thirty-nine years, he was brutally murdered by a mob June 27th, 1844.

Thus lived, suffered, toiled, and died, the martyr-prophet of the nineteenth century. Thus flashed athwart the spiritual darkness of his age, the light of the latter days. Even as in days of old the light shone in the darkness and the darkness comprehended it not. Contemplating his death the mind instinctively reverts to that scene, when the Savior suffered on Calvary, eighteen hundred years ago. Across the ages stride the footprints of the self-same spirit. Unconsciously are associated the death of the Reedemer and the matyrdom of His servant. Already the principles enunciated by Joseph Smith, have shaken the religious world from center to circumference. The ignorant may effect to scorn, yet the day is nigh, when America will be proud of her prophet son.

# LIST OF ILLUSTRATIONS.

# INDEX.

www.ingramcontent.com/pod-product-compliance
Lightning Source LLC
Chambersburg PA
CBHW030822270326
41928CB00007B/850